Thoughts are Things
& The God In You
by Prentice Mulford

Thoughts are Things

CONTENTS

The Material Mind Versus The Spiritual Mind

There belongs to every human being a higher self and a lower self--a self or mind of the spirit which has been growing for ages, and a self of the body, which is but a thing of yesterday. The higher self is full of prompting idea, suggestion and aspiration. This it receives of the Supreme Power. All this the lower or animal self regards as wild and visionary. The higher self argues possibilities and power for us greater than men and women now possess and enjoy. The lower self says we can only live and exist as men and women have lived and existed before us. The higher self craves freedom from the cumbrousness, the limitations, the pains and disabilities of the body. The lower self says that we are born to them, born to ill, born to suffer, and must suffer as have so many before us. The higher self wants a standard for right and wrong of its own. The lower self says we must accept a standard made for us by others--by general and long-held opinion, belief and prejudice.

"To thine own self be true" is an oft-uttered adage. But to which self? The higher or lower?

You have in a sense two minds—the mind of the body and the mind of the spirit.

Spirit is a force and a mystery. All we know or may ever know of it is that it exists, and is ever working and producing all results in physical things seen of physical sense and many more not so seen.

What is seen, of any object, a tree, an animal, a stone, a man is only a part of that tree, animal, stone, or man. There is a force which for a time binds such objects together in the form you see them. That force is always acting on them to greater or lesser degree. It builds up the flower to its fullest maturity. Its cessation to act on the flower or tree causes what we call decay. It is constantly changing the shape of all forms of what are called organized matter. An animal, a plant, a human being are not in physical shape this month or this year what they will be next month or next year.

This ever-acting, ever-varying force, which lies behind and, in a sense, creates all forms of matter we call Spirit.

To see, reason and judge of life and things in the knowledge of this force makes what is termed the "Spiritual Mind."

We have through knowledge the wonderful power of using or directing this force, when we recognize it, and know that it exists so as to bring us health, happiness and eternal peace of mind. Composed as we are of this force, we are ever attracting more of it to us and making it a part of our being.

With more of this force must come more and more knowledge. At first in our physical existances we allow it to work blindly. Then we are in the ignorance of that condition known as the material mind. But as mind through its growth or increase of this power becomes more and more awakened, it asks: "Why comes so much of pain, grief and disappointment in the physical life?" "Why do we seem born to suffer and decay"

That question is the first awakening cry of the spiritual mind, and an earnest question or demand for knowledge must in time be answered.

The material mind is a part of yourself, which has been appropriated by the body and educated by the body. It is as if you taught a child that the wheels of a steamboat made the boat move, and said nothing of the steam, which gives the real power. Bred in such ignorance, the child, should the wheels stop moving, would look no farther for the cause of their stoppage than to try to find where to repair them, very much as now so many depend entirely on repair of the physical body to ensure its healthy, vigorous movement, never dreaming that the imperfection lies in the real motive power—the mind.

The mind of the body or material mind sees, thinks and judges entirely from the material or physical standpoint. It sees in your own body all there is of you. The spiritual mind sees the body as an instrument for the mind or real self to use in dealing with material things. The material mind sees in the death of the body an end of all there is of you. The spiritual mind sees in the death of the body only the falling off from the spirit of a worn-out instrument. It knows that you exist as before only invisible to the physical eye. The material mind sees your physical strength as coming entirely from your muscles and sinews, and not from source without your body.

It sees in such persuasive power, as you may have with tongue or pen, the only force you possess for dealing with people to accomplish results The spiritual mind will know in time that your thought influences people for or against your interests, though their bodies are thousands of miles distant. The material mind does not regard its thought as an actual element as real as air or water. The spiritual mind knows that every one of its thousand daily secret thoughts are real things acting on the minds of the persons they are sent to. The spiritual mind knows that matter or the material is only an expression of spirit or force; that such matter is ever changing in accordance with the spirit that makes or externalizes itself in the form we call matter, and therefore, if the thought of health, strength and recuperation is constantly held to in the mind, such thought of health, strength and rejuvenation will express itself in the body, making maturity never ceasing, vigour never ending, and the keenness of every physical sense ever increasing.

The material mind thinks matter, or that which is known by our physical senses, to be the largest part of what exists. The spiritual mind regards matter as the coarser or cruder expression of spirit and the smallest part of what really exists. The material mind is made sad at the contemplation of decay. The spiritual mind attaches little importance to decay, knowing in such decay that spirit or the moving force in all things is simply taking the dead body or the rotten tree to pieces, and that it will build them up again as before temporarily into some other new physical form of life and beauty. The mind of the body thinks that its physical senses of seeing, hearing and feeling constitute all the senses you possess. The higher mind or mind of the spirit knows that it possesses other senses akin to those of physical sight and hearing, but more powerful and far reaching.

The mind of the body has been variously termed "the material mind," the "mortal mind " and the "carnal mind." All these refer to the same mind, or, in other words to that part of your real sell which has been educated in error by the body.

If you had been born and bred entirely among people who believed that the earth was a flat surface and did not revolve around the sun, you would in the earlier years of your physical growth believe as they did. Exactly in such fashion do you in your earlier years absorb the thought and belief of those nearest you, who think that the body is all there is of them, and judge of everything by its physical interpretation to them. This makes your material mind.

The material mind seeing, what seems to it, depth, dissolution and decay in all human organization, and ignorant of the fact that the real self or intelligence has in such seeming death only cast off a worn-out envelope, thinks that decay and death is the ultimate of all humanity. For such reason it cannot avoid a gloom or sadness coming of such error, which now pervades so much of human life at present. One result or reaction from such gloom born of hopelessness is a reckless spirit for getting every possible gratification and pleasure, regardless of right and justice so long as the present body lasts. This is a great mistake. All pleasure so gained cannot be lasting. It brings besides a hundredfold more misery and disappointment.

The spiritual mind teaches that pleasure is the great aim of existence. But it points out ways and means for gaining lasting happiness other than those coming of the teaching of the material mind. The spiritual mind, or mind opened to higher and newer forces of life, teaches that there is a law regulating the exercise of every physical sense. When we learn and follow this law, our gratifications and possessions do not prove sources of greater pain than happiness, as they do to so many.

By the spiritual mind is meant a clearer mental sight of things and forces existing both in us and the Universe, and of which the race for the most part has been in total ignorance. We have now but a glimpse of these forces, those of some being relatively a little clearer than those of others. But enough has been shown to convince a few that the real and existing causes for humanity's sickness, sorrow and disappointment have not in the past been seen at all. In other words, the race has been as children, fancying that the miller inside was turning the arms of the windmill, because some person had so told them. So taught their would remain in total ignorance that the wind was the motive power.

This illustration is not at all an overdrawn picture of the existing ignorance which rejects the idea that thought is an element all about us as plentiful as air, and that as blindly directed by individuals and masses of individuals in the domain of material mind or ignorance, it is turning the windmill's arms, sometimes in one direction, sometimes in another; sometimes with good and sometimes with evil results.

A suit of clothes is not the body that wears such suit. Yet the material mind reasons very much in this way. It knows of no such thing as clothing for the spirit, for it does not know that body and spirit are two distinct things. It reasons that the suit of clothing (the body) is all there is of the man or woman. When that man or woman tumbles to pieces through weakness, it sees only the suit of clothes so going to pieces, and all its efforts to make that man or woman stronger are put on the suit instead of making effort to reinforce the power within which has made the suit.

There are probably no two individuals precisely alike as regards the relative condition or action on them of their material and spiritual minds. With some the spiritual seems not at all awakened. With others it has begun to stretch and rub its eyes as a person does on physical awakening, when everything still appears vague and indistinct. Others are more fully awakened. They feel to greater or lesser extent that there are forces belonging to them before unthought of. It is with such that the struggle for mastery between the material and spiritual mind is likely to be most severe, and such struggle for a time is likely to be accompanied by physical disturbance, pain or lack of ease.

The material mind is, until won over and convinced of the truths, constantly received by the spiritual mind at war and in opposition to it The ignorant part of yourself dislikes very much to give up its long accustomed habits of thinking. Its costs a struggle in any case at first to own that we have been mistaken and give up views long held to.

The material mind wants to more on in a rut of life and idea, as it always has done, and as thousands are now doing. It dislikes change more and more as the crust of the old thought held from year to year grows more thickly over it. It wants to live on and on in the house it has inhabited for years; dress in the fashion of the past; go to business and return year in and year out at precisely the same hour. It rejects and despises after a certain age the idea of learning any new accomplishments, such as painting or music, whose greatest use is to divert the mind, rest it, and enable you to live in other departments of being, all this being apart from the pleasure also given you as the mind or spirit teaches the body more and more skill and expertness in the art you pursue.

The material mind sees as the principal use of any art only a means to bring money, and not in such art a means for giving variety to life, dispelling weariness, resting that portion of the mind devoted to other business, improving health and increasing vigour of mind and body. It holds to the idea of being "too old to learn."

This is the condition of so many persons who have arrived at or are past " middle age." They want to "settle down." They accept as inevitable the idea of "growing old." Their material mind tells them that their bodies must gradually weaken, shrink from the fullness and proportion of youth, decay and finally die.

Material minds say this always has been, and therefore always must be. They accept the idea wholly. They say quite unconsciously, "It must be."

To say a thing must be, is the very power that makes it. The material mind then sees the body ever as gradually decaying, even though it dislikes the picture, and puts it out of sight as much as possible. But the idea will recur from time to time as suggested by the death of their contemporaries, and as it does they think " must," and that state of mind indicated by the word "must" will inevitably bring material results in decay.

The spiritual or more enlightened mind says: "If you would help to drive away sickness, turn your thought as much as you can on health, strength and vigour, and on strong, healthy, vigorous material things, such as moving clouds, fresh breezes, the cascade, the ocean surge; on woodland scenes and growing healthy trees; on birds full of life and motion; for in so doing you turn on yourself a real current or this healthy life-giving thought, which is suggested and brought you by the thought of such vigorous, strong material objects.

And above all, try to rely and trust that Supreme Power which formed all these things and far more and which is the endless and inexhaustible part of your higher self or spiritual mind, and as your faith increases in this Power, so will your own power ever increase.

Nonsense! " says the ultra material mind. " If my body is sick, I must have something done to cure that body with things I can see and feel, and that is the only thing to be done. As for thinking, it makes no difference what I think, sick or well."

At present in such a case a mind whose sense of these truths new to it, has just commenced to be awakened, will, in many cases, allow itself to be for a time overpowered and ridiculed out of such an idea by its own material mind or uneducated part of itself; and in this it is very likely to be assisted by other material minds, who have not woke up at all to these truths, and who are temporarily all the stronger through the positiveness of ignorance. These are as people who cannot see as far ahead as one may with a telescope, and who may be perfectly honest in their disbelief regarding what the person with the telescope does see. Though such people do not speak a word or argue against the belief of the partly awakened mind, still their thought acts on such a mind as a bar or blind to these glimpses of the truth.

But when the spiritual mind has once commenced to awaken, nothing can stop its further waking, though the material may for a time retard it.

"Your real self may not at times be where your body is" says the spiritual mind. It is where your mind is—in the store, the office, the workshop, or with some person to whom you are strongly attached, and all of these may be in towns or cities far from the one your body resides in. Your real self moves with inconceivable rapidity as your thought moves. "Nonsense" says your material mind; "I myself am wherever my body is, and nowhere else"

Many a thought or idea that you reject as visionary, or as a whim or fancy, comes of the prompting of your spiritual mind. It is your material mind that rejects it.

No such idea comes but that there is a truth in it. But that truth we may not be able to carry out to a relative perfection immediately. Two hundred years ago some mind may have seen the use of steam as a motive power. But that motive power could not then have been carried out as it is today. A certain previous growth was necessary—a growth and improvement in the manufacture of iron, in the construction of roads, and in the needs of the people.

But the idea was a truth. Held to by various minds, it has brought steam as a motive power to its present relative perfection. It has struggled against and overcome every argument and obstacle placed in its way by dull, material, plodding minds. When you entertain any idea and say to yourself in substance: "Well, such a thing may be, though I cannot now see it" you remove a great barrier to the carrying out and realization by yourself of the new and strange possibilities in store for you.

The spiritual mind today sees belonging to itself a power for accomplishing any and all results in the physical world, greater than the masses dream of. It sees that as regards life's possibilities we are still in dense ignorance. It sees however, a few things—namely, perfect health, freedom from decay, weakness and death of the body, power of transit, travel and observation independent of the body, and methods for obtaining all needful and desirable material things through the action and working of silent mind or thought, either singly or in co-operation with others.

The condition of mind to be desired is the entire dominancy of the spiritual mind. But this does not imply dominancy or control in any sense of tyrannical mastership of the material mind by the spiritual mind. It does imply that the material mind will be swept away so far as its stubborn resistance and opposition to the promptings of the spiritual are concerned. It implies that the body will become the willing servant, or rather assistant of the spirit. It implies that the material mind will not endeavour to act itself up as the superior when it is only the inferior. It implies that state when the body will gladly lend its co-operation to all the desires of the spiritual mind.

Then all power can be given your spirit. Then no force need be expended in resisting the hostility of the material mind. Then all such force will be used to further our undertakings, to bring us material goods, to raise us higher and higher into realms of power, peace and happiness, to accomplish what now would be called miracles.

Neither the material mind nor the material body is to be won over and merged into the spiritual by any course of severe self censure or self denial, nor self punishment in expiation for sins committed, nor asceticism. That will only make you the more harsh, severe, bigoted and merciless, both to yourself and others. It is out of this perversion of the truth that have arisen such terms as " crucifying the body" and " subjugating the lower or animal mind." It is from this perversion that have come orders and associations of men and women who, going to another extreme, seek holiness in self denial and penance.

"Holiness" implies wholeness, or whole action of the spirit on the body, or perfect control by your spirit over a body, through knowledge and faith in our capacity to draw ever more and more from the Supreme Power.

When you get out of patience with yourself, through the aggressiveness of the material mind, through your frequent slips and falls into your besetting sins through periods of petulance or ill temper, or excess in any direction, you do no good, and only ill in calling or thinking for yourself hard names. You should not call yourself "a vile sinner" anymore than you would call any other person a "vile sinner," If you do, you put out in thought the "vile sinner" and make it temporarily a reality. If in your mental vision you teach yourself that you are "utterly depraved" and a "vile sinner," you are unconsciously making that your ideal, and you will unconsciously grow up to it until the pain and evil coming of such unhealthy growth either makes you turn back or destroys your body, For out of this state of mind, which in the past has been much inculcated, comes harshness, bigotry, lack of charity for others, hard, stern and gloomy and unhealthy views of life, and these mental conditions will surely bring physical disease.

When the material mind is put away, or, in other words, then we become convinced of the existence of these spiritual forces, both in ourselves, and outside of ourselves, and when we learn to use them rightly (for we are now and always have been using them in some way), then to use the words of Paul: " Faith is swallowed up in victory," and the sting and fear of death is removed. Life becomes then one glorious advance forward from the pleasure of today to the greater pleasure of tomorrow, and the phrase "to live" means only to enjoy.

Who Are Our Relations?

The man or woman who if most like you in tastes, motives, and habits of thought, and to whom you feel most attracted, may not be brother, sister, cousin, or any physical relative at all. But such person is to you a very near relation.

Your brothers or sisters may not be like you at all in mind, taste, and inclination. You may associate with them because they are members of the family, but were you not to know them as brothers, sisters, or other relatives, or were you to see elsewhere their exact counterparts in character, you might not like such counterparts at all.

Physical or " blood relationship" has very little bearing on the real or mental relationship. It is possible for a brother or sister, a father or mother to be very closely allied to you in thought and sympathy. Again, it is possible for a father or mother, brother or sister, to be very remote from you in thought and sympathy, and to live in a realm or atmosphere of thought very unlike yours.

You can live neither healthfully nor comfortably, unless with those whose thought-atmosphere (a literal emanation from them) is similar to your own. Physical relationship may or may not furnish such at atmosphere. Compel a labouring man whose thought goes little beyond his eating, drinking and daily round of work, to live exclusively with a company of artists and philosophers, seeing none of his own kind and order of thought, and that man's spirits would in time be depressed, and his health would suffer. The same law works when the superior mind is compelled to constant association with the inferior. Such may be your position among physical relatives.

Children live, thrive and are exhilarated by the thought-atmosphere emanating from their playmates. Cut them entirely off from such association and they droop. As a child, you lived upon this atmosphere of childhood; that is, you lived in the spiritual relationship of childhood, and regarding a certain playful thought nutriment, received it and also gave it to your playmates. You may wonder now why you cannot arouse the old feeling and exhilaration coming either from the associations of childhood or youth. It is because your spirit requires another thought food or atmosphere, which only another and probably higher order of mind can give. That received, and time would pass as quickly and pleasantly as it did with the associates of your earlier physical existence.

Those who can furnish it are your real relations. But such relationship cannot exist unless you can furnish them with the same quality of thought in return. The real or spiritual relations of many merchants, mechanics, and those of other callings, are their brother merchants, mechanics, or those of similar occupations. They prove this by their lives. They feel more at home with those whose business is like their own than they do in the places they may call home, to which they resort to eat, sleep, and spend often a tiresome Sunday, longing for Monday's coming, and the more welcome life of the market-stall and store. Because there they are amongst their real relations, and are being literally led and stimulated by the thought- atmosphere furnished them by these relatives, which they also furnish in turn.

Every order of mind or quality of thought must have association with a corresponding order of mind and quality of thought, or it will suffer. But "blood relationship" has little to do with furnishing such order of thought.

There is a vast amount of unconscious tyranny exercised through the ties of physical relationship. Children often, when grown up, place the mothers or fathers in their minds in a sphere and method of life where they may or may not care to belong. Then thought, seldom if ever expressed, runs in substance thus: "Mother is getting too old to wear bright colours. She must dress more subdued." " It is ridiculous for mother (if a widow) to marry again" (very hard cash reasons sometimes entering into this sentiment). " Mother, of course, does not want to enter into our gayer life, so she can stay at home and take care of the children." or, " It is time father retired from business," or, " Father's idea of marrying again is ridiculous."

No force is more subtle in its workings, nor more powerful to bring results for good or ill than the steady output of thought from one or several minds combined, on one person to effect some desired result, and whether this is done intelligently and consciously, or blindly, the force works the same result.

Now a continual flow of this kind of thought, coming from, possibly, three or four minds to whom "mother" was instrumental in furnishing new bodies, and continually directed on "mother," is a very powerful force to direct and keep her exactly where the children find it most convenient to have her. The whole conventional current of thought also flows as an aid in this direction. "Mother," says this unspoken sentiment, "must of course grow old, retire gradually from a more active and gayer life, and retire also to a corner of the household, to associate with other shelved and declining parents, and he useful as a general upper nurse in times of sickness or other family emergency." Through the action on her on these minds, many mothers cease to have any privileges as individuals, and eventually do exactly as their children desire.

Possibly it is here remarked or thought, "But should I not go to my mother or other near relative with my cares and trials, and receive her help, as I have always been in the habit of doing? Ought not those of my own family, above all others, to help me in time of need?"

Certainly, if the mother or any of your physical relatives are glad and anxious so to do. Certainly, if such service from a relative comes directly from the heart and is not impelled by the sentiment taking sometimes this form of unspoken expression: "I suppose I must do this because it is my brother, or my son, or other physical relative who asks it." Asks it? Many, many are these services which are unconsciously demanded, rather than asked, in these cases. Loads are piled upon relatives simply because they are relatives. Favours in money—in the endorsement of notes, are in a sense exacted through sympathy of relatives. Support, food, shelter, maintenance, are expected from relatives when it cannot be procured elsewhere. Hospitality is expected from relatives, when to expect hospitality is to make such entertainment the result of a demand. Presents are expected from relatives, when to expect a gift makes it rather an extortion.

Real gifts are always surprises. No one expects a surprise since expectation destroys surprise. Relatives visit and "camp down" on other relatives simply because they are relatives, and a vast amount of grudging, grumbling, but unspoken thought is always going out when relatives use each other's houses to save hotel bills.

No real or lasting good comes of any gift bestowed on another unless the heart goes with it, and its bestowal is to the giver an act of unalloyed pleasure. Because something else goes with the material gift, the food, the shelter, the loan, which though not seen, and little known, is more important than the form itself. That is the thought which goes with it, That thought strongly affects, for good or ill, the person who receives the gift. If, as giving within your means, you bestow the merest trifle in money upon a person in need, and the thought that goes with it is not only the most sincere desire to help that person, but you feel a keen sense of pleasure in giving such help, then you throw upon that person a certain thought-element which will never leave them, and benefit them eternally and in proportion to the quality, power and force of your thought. Then you do far more than relieve their present physical necessity. You give them a certain amount of spiritual power. Your wish that their power may be so developed and increased as to enable them to live above beggary, and draw to themselves the goods of this earth (as all will and must, when grown to a certain stature in spiritual power), is a great help for them in time to acquire such power. You have sent and sown in them a seed of thought which will take root and bear fruit at some period of their real or spiritual existence.

But if you give grudgingly, if you give under any sort of compulsion, if you give food, shelter, clothing, money, anything, only because circumstances compel you so to do, or because people might talk unfavourably of you for not giving, or because other people are so giving, then your gift does relatively little good, no matter on whom bestowed, be it even mother, father, brother, sister, son or daughter.

You relieve, then, only a physical necessity, and that only for a time. You may possibly feed a body, shelter it, clothe it. But you do not, and cannot feed properly the spirit that uses that body if the thought going with your gift is not that of the most perfect willingness and hearty pleasure in relieving that body's necessities. The grudging thought accompanying the gift, the thought common to that position when the recipient of the gift (no matter how near the relationship) is endured rather than enjoyed, the thought accompanying any gift to any person, or relative, that is given principally because custom and public opinion require it, or because of the recipient's importunity, is a great damage both to giver and taker. It is the sending to the one who receives a current of thought, evil in its character and result. It brings back to the giver from the one who takes a response in thought of like nature, and this also is harmful. Because, if you receive a gift which you have in any way extorted your feeling for the giver is not that of warm, glowing gratitude, but something quite different.

The Christ of Judea, when commending the widow who cast her mite into the treasury, did so in our estimation and as seen in this light, not merely because she gave in proportion to her material means, but because he saw that her thought of desire to help in whatever way help was needed, going with that mite, was far more heartfelt and genuine than that of richer people who cast in larger sums, but cast in also with them a lower character of thought and motive. He saw, also, that the woman's thought was actually doing far more to help than that of the others, for it was purer, less mixed with lower motive and therefore far the stronger.

"Is it not my duty," some may ask, "to feed, clothe, shelter, and support a very near relative or parent, if helpless, in their old age?"

The term "doing from a sense of duty" does not always imply that the thing done, be it the person helped or the patient nursed through sickness, is done from the impulse of love for that person or love for the doing. It is sometimes done mechanically, or with dislike for the doing. It is sometimes a forced and painful performance. For such reason little good is done, for if physical necessities are temporarily relieved, spiritual necessities are not, and unless the spiritual portion of our natures is fed there can be no permanent relief or good done the physical. Parents who in old age are supported by their children merely from a sense of duty, have sometimes their spirits wounded and starved—wounded, because they feel they are endured encumbrances—-starved, because no real love goes with the gift or service done by these children. Children who come into the world unwelcomed by the parent and are brought up only because custom, conventionality and public opinion demand their support from that parent, are most unfortunate, and suffer from the blight and starvation thereby caused their spirits. Genuine heartfelt love is literally life giving, and if received by the child is for it a source of cheer, health, strength, and activity.

There is a certain trained conscience whose basis of education is fear of public or private opinion. This sometimes really impels acts which are said to be done from a "sense of duty." If public opinion should suddenly change, and cast no censure at all on the person who refused to support very near relatives in want or old age, a proportion of such relatives would probably go to the poor-house, and the son or daughter who sent them there would be acting out their real natures, and not feigning a sentiment they did not possess.

Mothers sometimes say, "I don't care what becomes of me, so that my children are well brought up and educated." A mother should care a great deal for her own cultivation. If her cultivation and growth in wisdom are checked, that of her children will be checked. It will be checked if she sinks herself in her endeavour to favour her children. A genuine mother will continually compel the admiration and respect, as well as love of her children. Such admiration and respect can be compelled only by a woman who knows the world, has standing and position in it and is ever pushing forward to more commanding place and position. Such admiration and respect from son or daughter cannot be compelled by the mother who retires to a household corner, becomes a cross between upper nurse and governess, neglects her dress and personal appearance, and teaches her children that she is at their disposal and use in all family emergencies, real or fancied. For this very reason are many mothers ignored, snubbed, and ridiculed by their grown-up children.

If mothers so sink themselves, as they falsely imagine, to benefit their children, they pay in cases a terrible penalty. If you allow your will constantly to be overborne by another; if you give up your own preferences and inclinations, and become only another's echo; if you live just as others desire, you will lose more and more, for this existence, the power of self-assertion; you will absorb so much of the other mind and thought about you as to become a part of that mind, and so act in accordance even with its silent will and unspoken desire; you will fossilize, and sink into a hopeless servitude; you will lose more and more of both physical and mental power for doing anything; you will become the chimney-corner encumbrance, the senile parent, the helpless old man or woman, endured rather than loved.

This, in many instances, has been the effect of the grown-up children's minds upon a parent. It is the silent force of those minds, continually working on that of the parent, which helps to break the parent down physically, and the decay and mental weakness, commonly charged to "advancing years," is due in part to the injurious effect of a mind or group of minds, seeking to usurp and overpower another. This evil is done unconsciously. The son wishes to manage the farm. His will may be strong. He gains power step by step. He takes as rights what at first he took only by a father's permission or as privileges. He goes on step by step, having his way in all things, great and small, perhaps being aided by others of the children, using their silent force in the same direction. And this may be a combined force almost impossible for one person to withstand if continually exposed to it. It is a steady, incessant pressure, all in one direction. It works night and day. It works all the more efficaciously, because the parent so exposed to it is utterly ignorant of such a force and its operation upon him. He finds himself growing weak. He becomes inert. He lacks his old vigour, and thinks it is through the approach of old age.

I knew a man over seventy years of age and as sound, active and vigorous in mind and body as one of forty. He had organized and built up a large business. His several children at last took it into their heads that it was time " father retired from business." Henceforth, the thought spoken and unspoken, bearing month in and month out on father from the children, was this desire and demand that he should retire from business. Confiding his situation to a friend, he said, "Why should I retire from business? I live in it, I like it, and so far as I can see, am able to conduct it properly." But the persistent demand and force brought to bear on him from these foes of his own blood and household were too great to withstand. He did retire. The sons and daughters were satisfied. The father soon commenced to decline in health. He lived about two years afterwards, and one of his last remarks was, "My children have killed me."

"Ought I not to love my children above all others" asks one. The term " ought " has no application to the nature of love. Love goes where it will, and to whom it will, and where it is attracted. You cannot force yourself to love anything or anybody. There have been parents who had no real love for their children, and children who had no real love for their parents. Neither party can be blamed for this. They were lacking in the capacity for loving. They were born so lacking. They are no more to be censured for such deficiency than you would censure a person for being born blind or cripple.

Some parents fancy they love their children, yet do not. A father who loses his temper and beats his son does not really love that son. It would be better to say that he loved to beat him, or tyrannize over him. Government in the family is necessary; bur no sound, loving government is administered on a basis of anger and irascibility. Parents sometimes interfere and seriously affect the future of a child by opposing its desires in the choice of a profession. The parent may be prejudiced against certain walks in life. The child may wish to follow one of these walks. It meets a bitter, uncompromising opposition on the parent's part. There is no reasoning, discussion, or counselling in the matter—nothing but a stern, positive "No." Such sentiment and act are not impelled by love for the child on the parent's part. They are impelled by the parent's love for his or her own opinion and a love of tyranny.

Parents sometimes forget that after the child emerges from the utter physical and mental helplessness of infancy, it is becoming more and more an individual. As an individual it may show decided tastes, preferences and inclinations in some direction. No parent and no person can break or alter these tastes and preferences. No one can make that child's mind over into something else. For the child's mind as we call it, is really a mind or spirit, which has lived other physical lives from infancy to maturity, if not to old age, and as it comes into possession of its new body, and acquires a relative control over that body, it will begin to act out the man or woman as it was in its former life, and that may be a man or woman very closely related to the parent or hardly related at all. But in any event, the parent is dealing with an individual, who is growing more and more into tastes, preferences, and traits of character which belong to and are a part of it These must have expression. They will have expression in mind or spirit, whether allowed to physically or not. If the boy is ever longing to go to sea, and the parent forbids, the boy is on the sea in mind; and if so in mind, it is far better that his body should follow, for there is only damage when mind and body are not working in correspondence together. If the mother refuse to allow the boy to go to sea because she fears its dangers for him, still she is loving her own fears and her own way, too, more than she does her son.

The parent sometimes usurps a complete tyranny, not only over the child's body, but over its mind. The child's tastes, inclination, tendencies and preferences are held as of no importance whatever. If the boy wants to be a sailor, and the parent wants him something else—that something else the parent may insist that he shall be, but does he succeed? Let the host of mediocrity in all callings in the land answer. And mediocrity means the mechanical following of any pursuit in which there it no live interest.

More than this; where a body is compelled to do one thing, or live in a certain way, and the mind longs to live in another, there is a force set in motion which in many cases tears mind and body apart; and parents sometimes grieve over the loss of a child, when they are responsible for the death of its body from this cause.

How long, then, should parental control continue over the child—or, rather, over a spirit for which you have been an agency for furnishing with a new body? Is it unreasonable to say that such control should not continue after such body, emerging from the helplessness of infancy, shall have acquired such control of its organization as shall enable it to meet all physical demands and necessities? To go beyond this, and give food, clothes, shelter, maintenance, to a person, is doing him or her a great injustice, and even cruelty. In so doing you do not grant exercise to those faculties which must be used in coping successfully with the world. You make the children the less fitted to be self-sustaining, and earn their own living. You teach them to lie in a soft, luxurious bed, when they should be out in the world exercising and making more strong and dexterous their powers, both of mind and body.

Parents sometimes make themselves unjustly responsible, and inflict needless mental suffering on themselves, for the errors and tendencies of their children. A son or daughter takes a wrong course—or, rather, let us put it, a course where the evil is more prominent or more opposed to conventional ideas of propriety than other habits more tolerated and deemed reputable, but which may be the subtle, and for the most part unknown, sources of as great ills as those condemned by society. A son takes to drink or reckless associates and commits some crime. The parent condemns herself for not having looked more carefully after her boy. She may accuse herself as having been, through her neglect, the prime agency for her son's misdeeds.

Madame, you blame yourself far too much. You did not make that son or daughter's character. It was made long before that spirit had the use of its last new body. What traits, what imperfections were very prominent in its last existence, will appear in its next. If that was a thieving spirit before, it will probably show thieving tendencies now. If it was gross, animal and gluttonous, then similar tendencies will show themselves now. You, if grown to a more refined plane of thought, may do much to modify and lessen these tendencies.

But all that you will do in this respect will be done through the silent force and action of your superior thought on your child's mind. It will not be done through a great deal of verbal counsel or physical punishment or discipline.

Whatever a mind is on entering on a new physical experience, whatever imperfection belongs to it, must appear and be acted out and beget pain and punishment of some kind, until that spirit sees clearly for itself, how, through its errors, it brings these punishments on itself. These lessons can only be learned when that person has full freedom, so far as parental control goes, to live as it pleases. You may for a time control such a life, and make it externally live as you please. But such external life is only a veneer, if the mind be full of lower tastes and inclinations. The sooner these are lived out, the sooner will that person learn the real law, which inflicts pains and penalties for breaking its unchangeable rules, and the sooner will it know the happiness which comes of living in accordance with Its rules. That every spirit must do for him or herself.

A parent may mould a false character for a child. It may teach indirectly, through the effect of its own mental condition operating on the child, how to feign what the world calls goodness, how it may seem, as regards outward conduct, to be what it is not at all in secret tendency and inclination,—how, in brief, to be a hypocrite.

No person is really reformed by another, in the sense such a term is sometimes used. Reform must come from within. It must be self-sustaining. It must not depend wholly on another's presence or influence. If it does, it is only a temporary reform. It will fail when the influence of the person on whom it depends is removed. We hear sometimes the assertion, "such or such a person's wife has been the making of him" (meaning the husband). By the way, why do we never hear of the man's being the making of his wife?

A man may be prevented from intemperance, or he may continually be braced up to meet the world through his wife's influence and mental power. But if in such reform he relies entirely upon her; if he cannot sustain himself without her continual presence and prompting, his is no lasting reformation, and he is also a very heavy and damaging load for her to carry. It is a one-sided piece of business when one person must supply all the sustaining force for two, and if this is persisted in, the wife, or whoever so supplies it, will at last sink under such burden, and there will be two wrecked lives instead of one. No person can "make another," in the highest sense. But one person having the superior mind, can, if in a very close and long-continued association with one weaker, give temporarily to the weaker their very life and force, if their desire it very strong to help the weaker. If it be the husband who so receives of the wife, and is so dependent on the wife then he does not represent any character of his own. He represents and is clothed temporarily with his wife's character, or as much of it as he can appropriate. If she dies, or is removed from him, then he relapses and sinks into his real self, unless he is resolved to be self-sustaining, and evolve force out of himself instead of using another's. If she continues to supply him, she is only sustaining his temporary character, which cannot last when its source of supply is removed, and in such continuance she will certainly in time exhaust herself.

Parents often unconsciously teach their children to lie down upon them, to depend upon them too long for moral support. The result of this error is that then the parent's life is dragged out, through carrying so heavy a load, the child ceases to have any genuine love for its parent. You may pity what is decrepit, weak, and shattered. Love it you cannot. Love is based on admiration, and admiration is not compelled by decay.

The tendency called instinct, which impels the mother bird to turn its young out of the nest, so soon as they have sufficient strength to fly, and the animal in weaning its young to turn them adrift and leave them to shift for themselves, is founded on the natural and divine laws. We may say it is the custom of the brutes and is therefore "brutal." But would it be a kindness for the bird to encourage the young to stay in the nest where it could not gain strength, and when a few weeks will bring the storms and severity of winter, which the parent bird itself cannot withstand? Again, the parent, be it bird, animal, or human mother, needs after these periods of bringing their young into the world and rearing them, a season of entire rest and recuperation, and the duration of such resting season should be proportionate to the complexity of the organization and the force expended by such organization. During such periods, the parent should be freed from any and all demands from the child. Birds and animals in their natural or wild life take such periods of rest. But thousands of human mothers are never free from the demands of their children, until worn out they drop into their graves. They should be as free, so far as their children a concerned, as they were in girlhood, and before they became mothers. Motherhood is a most necessary and an indispensable phase of existence for ripening and developing qualities. But no one experience should be followed and dwelt in forever. Life in its more perfected state will be full of alterations—not a rut, into which if you are once set you must continually travel.

If human children remain with the mother years after attaining what may be termed a responsible age; if they always look to her for aid, advice, sympathy, and assistance; if the mother allows herself to become the family leaning-post, she may also be repeating the one-sided business of supplying too much force to others and getting none back. She may be practising a false and injurious species of motherhood because it is exacted, begged, or dragged from her. She may be robbing herself of the new life which awaits her, when the brood is reared and their wings are self-sustaining. She is helping the children to make her a feeble, witless "old woman."

Perhaps one remarks: " If your suggestion was literally followed, the streets would be full of children turned by parents out of their homes and unable to provide for themselves." So they would. I argue here no literal following of the example set by bird and beast. It would be a great injustice. No custom, when followed for ages, even if based in error, can be suddenly changed without disturbance, injustice, and wrong. Yet it is worth our while to study this principle that we find in nature, from the tree that casts adrift the ripe acorn, to the bird or animal that casts adrift the relatively ripened young. Neither acorn, bird nor animal, when cast off or weaned, ever returns to the parent for self-sustaining power. Such power, in these cases, is only given by the parent until the new organization is strong enough to absorb and appropriate of the elements about it, absorb of earth and sunshine, or flesh or grain, the nourishment necessary to its support.

Are not our streets today full of grown-up children quite unable to provide for themselves? Do not thousands leave parental homes with no self-sustaining power, who are all through life unable to feed, clothe, and shelter themselves, save by long hours of drudging labour at the lowest wages? Does not this life of drudgery exhaust and cut them off prematurely? Are there not thousands of daughters all over the land who will become "old maids," and whose parents will not permit them, were they so disposed, to go out in the world and take their chances? These are the birds cuddled in the nest, until their wings, denied exercise, lose at last all power or prompting for flight, and whose mouths, though they become grown-up birds, are trained only to open and receive the morsels dropped in them.

Thought Currents

We need to be careful of what we think and talk. Because thought runs in currents as real as those of air and water. Of what we think and talk we attract to us a like current of thought. This acts on mind or body for good or ill.

If thought was visible to the physical eye we should see its currents flowing to and from people. We should see that persons similar in temperament, character and motive are in the same literal current of thought. We should see that the person in a despondent and angry mood was in the same current with others despondent or angry, and that each one in such moods serves as an additional battery or generator of such thought and is strengthening that particular current. We should see these forces working in similar manner and connecting the hopeful, courageous and cheerful, with all others hopeful, courageous and cheerful.

When you are in low spirits or "blue" you have acting on you the thought current coming from all others in low spirits. You are in oneness with the despondent order of thought. The mind is then sick. It can be cured, but a permanent cure cannot always come immediately when one has long been in the habit of opening the mind to this current of thought.

In attracting to us the current of any kind of evil, we become for a time one with evil. In the thought current of the Supreme Power for good we may become more and more as one with that power, or in Biblical phrase "One with God." That is the desirable thought current for us to attract.

If a group of people talk of any form of disease or suffering, of death-bed scenes and dying agonies, if they cultivate this morbid taste for the unhealthy and ghastly, and it forms their staple topics of conversation, they bring in themselves a like current of thought full of images of sickness, suffering and things revolting to a healthy mind. This current will act on them, and eventually bring them disease and suffering in some form.

If we are talking much of sick people or are much among them and thinking of them, be our motive what it may, we shall draw on ourselves a current of sickly thought, and its ill results will in time materialize itself in out bodies. We have far more to do to save ourselves than is now realized.

When men talk business together they attract a business current of idea and suggestion. The better they agree the more of this thought current do they attract and the more do they receive of idea and suggestion for improving and extending their business. In this way does the conference or discussion among the leading members of the company or corporation create the force that carries their business ahead.

Travel in first-class style, put up at first-class hotels and dress in apparel "as costly as your purse can buy," without running into the extreme of foppishness. In these things you find aids to place you in a current of relative power and success. If your purse does not now warrant such expenditure, or you think it does not, you can commence so living in mind. This will make you take the first steps in this direction. Successful people in the domain of finance unconsciously live up to this law. Desire for show influences some to this course. But there is another force and factor which so impels them. That is a wisdom of which their material minds are scarcely conscious. It is the wisdom of the spirit telling them to get in the thought current of the successful, and by such current be borne to success. It is not a rounded-out success, but good is far as it goes.

If our minds are, from what is falsely called economy, ever set on the cheap—cheap lodgings, cheap food and cheap fares, we get in the thought current of the cheap, the slavish and the fearful. Our views of life and our plans will be influenced and warped by it. It paralyzes that courage and enterprise implied in the old adage "Nothing ventured nothing gained." Absorbed in this current and having it ever acting on you, it is felt immediately when you come into the presence of the successful and causes them to avoid you. They feel in you the absence of that element which brings them their relative success. It acts as a barrier, preventing the flow to you of their sympathy. Sympathy is a most important factor in business. Despite opposition and competition, a certain thought current of sympathy binds the most successful together. The mania for cheapness lies in the thought current of fear and failure. The thought current of fear and failure, and the thought current of dash, courage and success will not mingle nor bring together the individuals who are in these respective streams of thought. They antagonize, and between the two classes of mind is built a barrier more impenetrable than walls of stone.

Live altogether in any one idea, any one "reform" and you get into the thought current of all other minds who are carrying that idea to extremes. There is no "reform" but what can be pushed too far. The harm of such extreme falls on the person who so pushes it. It warps mind, judgment and reason all on one side. It makes fanatics, bigots, cranks and lunatics, whether the idea involves an art or study, a science, a "reform" or a "movement." It connects the extremists of all people in such order and current of mind, no matter what their specialties may be. Such people often end in becoming furious haters of all who differ with them and in so hating expend their force in tearing themselves to pieces. The safe side lies in calling daily for the thought current of wisdom from the Infinite Mind.

When that wisdom is more invoked our "reforms" and organizations "for the good of the whole" will not run into internal wrangles almost as soon as they organize. As now conducted the thought current of hatred of and antagonism to the "oppressor" and monopolist is admitted at their birth.

This very force breeds quarrels and dissensions among the members. It is force used to tear down instead of build up. It is like taking the fire used to generate steam in the boilers and scattering it throughout the building.

When people come together and in any way talk out their ill-will towards others they are drawing to themselves with ten-fold power an injurious thought current. Because the more minds united on any purpose the more power do they attract to effect that purpose. The thought current so attracted by those chronic complainers, grumblers and scandal mongers, will injure their bodies. Because whatever thought is most held in mind is most materialized in the body. If we are always thinking and talking of people's imperfections we are drawing to us ever of that thought current, and thereby incorporating into ourselves those very imperfections.

We have said in previous books that "Talk Creates Force," and that the more who talk in sympathy the greater is the volume and power of the thought current generated and attracted for good or ill. A group of gossips who can never put their heads together without raking over the faults of the absent are unconsciously working a law with terrible results to themselves.

Gossip is fascinating. There is an exhilaration in scandal and the raking over of our friend's or neighbour's or enemy's faults is almost equal to that produced by champagne. But in the end we pay dearly for these pleasures.

If but two people were to meet at regular intervals and talk of health, strength and vigour of body and mind, at the same time opening their minds to receive of the Supreme the best idea as to the ways and means for securing these blessings, they would attract to them a thought current of such idea. If these two people or more kept up these conversations on these subjects at a regular time and place, and found pleasure in such communings, and they were not forced or stilted; if they could carry them on without controversy, and enter into them without preconceived idea, and not allow any shade of tattle or tale-bearing, or censure of others to drift into their talk, they would be astonished at the year's end at the beneficial results to mind and body. Because in so doing and coming together with a silent demand of the Supreme to get the best idea, they would attract to them a current of Life-giving force.

Let two so commence rather than more. For even two persons in the proper agreement and accord to bring the desired results are not easy to find. The desire for such meetings must be spontaneous, and any other motive will bar out the highest thought current for good.

The old-fashioned revival meeting, or camp meeting, through the combined action and desire of a number of minds brought a thought current, causing for the time the ecstasy, fervour and enthusiasm which characterized those gatherings The North American Indian worked himself into the frenzy of his war dance by a similar law. He brought to him by force of united desire a thought element and current which stimulated and even intoxicated him. His sole desire was to bring on him this mental intoxication. The more minds so working in the same vein, the quicker came the desired result.

The real orator in his effort draws to him a current of thought, which as sent again from him to his audience, thrills them. So does the inspired actor or actress. They bring a higher and more powerful element of thought to themselves first, and this flowing through them acts on the audience afterwards.

If you dwell a great deal on your own faults you will by the same laws attract more and more of their thought current, and so increase those faults. It is enough that you recognize in yourself those faults. Don't be always saying of yourself, "I am weak or cowardly or ill-tempered or imprudent," Draw to yourself rather the thought current of strength, courage, even temper, prudence and all other good qualities. Keep the image of these qualities in mind and you make them a part of yourself.

You have sometimes been beset, absorbed, and even annoyed for days in the thought of the suit of clothes you wanted to buy, the cut, colour and fashion of a dress, the selection of a bonnet, or cravat, until you were nothing in thought but clothes, hat, bonnet, dress, cravat or some other detail of life. You may not have been able to make up your mind what you should buy, and have then possibly been tossed about mentally on the billows of indecision for days. You have then got into the thought current of thousands of other minds continually in this mood of thought.

The surest way for a young woman to become ugly is to be discontented, peevish, cross, complaining and envious of others. Because in these states of mind she is drawing to her the invisible substance of thought, which acts on and injures her body. It ruins the complexion, makes lines and creases in the face, sharpens the nose and transforms the face of youth into that of the shrew in very quick time.

I am not moralizing here or saying: "You ought not to do thus and so." It is simply cause and result. Put your face in the fire, and it is scarred and disfigured, because of an element acting on it. Put your mind in the fire of ill-will, envy or jealousy, and it is also scarred, seamed and disfigured, because of an element as real as fire, though invisible, acting on it.

All things that are evil and imperfect, such as disagreeable traits of character in others—things unpleasant to hear or look upon should be gotten out of our minds as quickly as possible. Otherwise if dwelt upon, they attract of their thought current. They will then become permanent spiritual fixtures, and these will in time materialize themselves into corresponding physical fixtures. If we are always keeping in mind the person doing some wrong thing, we are the more apt to do that very thing ourselves.

Let us endeavour, then, with the help of the Supreme Power, to get into the thought current of things that are healthy, natural, strong and beautiful. Let us try to avoid thoughts of disease, of suffering, of deformity, of faultiness. A field of waving grain or the rolling surf is better to contemplate than to pore over the horrors of a railway accident. We do not realize how much we are depressed physically and mentally by the incessant feast of horrors prepared for us by the daily press. We invoke in their perusal a thought current, filled with things and images of horror and suffering. We bring ourselves in this way in connection and one-ness with all other morbid and diseased mind, which lives and revels in this current. it leads not to life, but to disease and death. Neither others nor yourself are one particle aided by your knowing of every fire, explosion, murder, theft or crime which the newspapers chronicle every twenty-fours hours.

  If we read boots written by cynical, sarcastic minds, who are so warped as to be able to see only the faults of others, and at last unable to see good anywhere, we bring on ourselves their unhealthy thought current, and are one with it. The arrow always tipped with ill-nature and sarcasm is deadliest to him who sends it. In other words, the man who is ever inviting and cultivating this thought current, is inviting the unrest, disease and misfortune it will assuredly bring to him, and when we get too much into his mind we invite similar results.

  You may be neat, careful and methodical in your habits, exact and elaborate in your work, yet if you associate closely with those who are careless and slovenly you may find in yourself a tendency to be also careless and slovenly, and a difficulty in resuming and carrying out your former neat, methodical and orderly methods. Because you have not only absorbed of the careless mind, or the mind lacking patience to do anything reposefully, but the fragment of such mind so absorbed is acting as a magnet in attracting to you its like thought current.

  When an evil is known it is half cured. Bear in mind when you are in any unpleasant frame of mind that a thought current of such disagreeable mood is acting on you. Bear in mind that you are then one in a sort of electrical connection with many other sickly and morbid minds, all generating and sending unpleasant thought to each other. The next thing to be done is to pray or demand to get out of this current of evil thought. You cannot do this wholly of your own individual effort. You must demand of the Supreme Power to divert it from you.

  We can more and more invite the thought current of things that are lively, sprightly and amusing. Life should be full of playfulness. Continued seriousness is but a few degrees removed front gloom and melancholy. Thousands live too much in the thought current of seriousness. Faces which wear a smiling expression are scarce. Some never smile at all. Some have forgotten how to smile, and it actually hurts them to smile, or to see others do so. Sickness and disease are nursed into fresher and fresher activity by the serious mood of mind. Habit continually strengthens the sad capacity of dwelling on the malady, which may be the merest trifle at first. People get so much in this current that woeful diseases are manufactured out of some trifling irritation in some part of the body.

Many material things are helps to divert a thought current acting disagreeably on you. You may have daily a set of disagreeable symptoms. They may seem to come as adjuncts to the daily routine of life. The breakfast table, the furniture, the conversation and even the persons immediately about you seem to recall them. Travel sometimes banishes them entirely. The sight of different surroundings diverts that particular thought current. Material remedies may temporarily effect the same result. So may any sudden change of life or occupation. But all these are secondary aids to the Supreme Power.

The thought current of fear is everywhere. All humanity fears something—disease, death, loss of fortune, loss of friends, loss of something. Everyone has his or her pet fear. It extends to the most trivial details of life. The streets are full of people who, if fearing nothing else, fear they won't catch a train or the next street car. The more sensitive you are to the impress of thought, the more liable are you to be affected by this thought current of fear until your spirit, by constant demand of the Supreme Power, builds up for itself an armour of thought positive to this current, and one which will deny it access. You can commence this building in saying, whenever you are affected in the way above mentioned, or in any disagreeable fashion, "I refuse to accept this thought and the mental condition it has brought on me which affects my body." You commence then to turn aside the thought current of evil.

Everyone has some pet fear—some disease they may never have had, but always dreaded— something they are in special fear of losing. Some trifle, even but a word or sentence uttered by another, brings this pet fear to the mind. Instantly through long habit the minds reverts to this fear. Instantly it opens to it, and the whole thought, volume and current rushes to and acts on them. It acts and vibrates on that particular chord of your nature, which for years has sounded your pet weakness.

Then in some way the body is affected disagreeably. There are myriads of different symptoms. The body may become weak and tremulous. There may be loss of appetite, tremulousness, a dry tongue, a bad taste in the mouth, weakness in the joints, drowsiness, difficulty of concentrating the mind on your business and many other disagreeable sensations.

Such symptoms are often classed as " malaria." In a sense the name is a correct one. Only in very many of these cases it is a bad atmosphere or current of thought which is acting on our minds instead of the fancied bad material atmosphere. Unquestionably an atmosphere full of vegetable or animal decomposition will affect many people. But some live for years in the midst of stagnant pools and swamps who never have malaria. Others far removed from such locations on high and dry ground do have it. They hare taken on a thought current of fear.

Place yourself in a house where there has recently been a panic or scare, though you may know nothing of it. You were well and strong the day before. You arise in the morning, and soon this whole train of disagreeable sensations affects you, because the house or place is saturated with a thought current of fear. Put a fear on city, town or country of some deadly epidemic or some great calamity, and hundreds of the more sensitive who may have no fear of that epidemic or calamity are still affected by it disagreeably. That thought current affects them in their particular a weak spot. A fanatic predicts some great catastrophe. The sensational newspapers take up the topic, ventilate it, affect to ridicule, but still write about it. This sets more minds to thinking and more people to talking. The more talk the more of this injurious force is generated. As a result thousands of people are affected by it unpleasantly, some in one way, some in another, because the whole force of that volume of fear is let loose upon them. Some are killed outright. Entirely unaware of the cause, they open their minds more and more to it, dwell on it in secret, put out no resisting thought until at last the spirit, unable longer to carry such a load, snaps the link which connects it with the body.

The more impressionable you are to the thought about you the more are you liable to be thus affected. But you can train your mind to shut out this thought. You can gradually train it to bar tightly this door to weakness, and keep open only the one to strength. You can do this by cultivating the mood of drawing to yourself and keeping in the mood and current of thought coming of God or the Supreme Power for good.

Impressionability or capacity to receive thought is source either of strength or weakness. Fine-grained, sensitive, highly developed minds today often carry the weakest bodies, because through ignorance they are always inviting some of these currents of evil without any knowledge of their existence or the means of throwing them off. They are ignorantly either courting or exposing themselves to such current. Improper individual association is one chief source of such exposure.

The finer feminine organization is more sensitive to every shade and ray of thought about it, good or bad. Men absorbed in their business generate for a time a certain positiveness which throws off the fear current. But this positiveness cannot always last.

Women from this cause often suffer a thousandfold more in the privacy of their homes than men are aware of. The average man defines it as " woman's way," and wonders why she is so full of " nervousness," " vapours," "notions," and ill-health.

As you place your reliance on the Infinite Mind to bring you out of all these agencies for ill, that mind in some way will bring many material aids to help you out. That mind will suggest medicines and foods and surroundings and changes, not only to help you temporarily, but permanently, so that when you are cured you are cured for all time. A cheerful, buoyant, hopeful mind (and no mind is cheerful, hopeful and buoyant without being nearer the Infinite than one that is depressed, sour and gloomy), be that the mind of your doctor, or your friend, will help you to get out of the injurious thought current. Regard such mind as a help from the Infinite. But don't put your whole trust in that individual. Put the great trust in the Supreme Power which has sent to you the individual as a temporary aid or crutch until your spiritual limbs are strong enough to bear you.

The more you get into the thought current coming from the Infinite Mind, making yourself more and more a part of that mind (exactly as you may become a part of any vein of low, morbid, unhealthy mind in opening yourself to that current), the quicker are you freshened, and renewed physically and mentally. You become continually a newer being. Changes for the better come quicker and quicker. Your power increases to bring results. You lose gradually all fear as it is proven more and more to you that when you are in the thought current of Infinite good there is nothing to fear. You realize more and more clearly that there is a great power and force which cares for you. You are wonderstruck at the fact that when your mind is set in the right direction all material things come to you with very little physical or external effort. You wonder then at man's toiling and striving, fagging himself literally to death, when through such excess of effort he actually drives from him the rounded-out good of health, happiness and material prosperity all combined.

You will see in this demand for the highest good that you are growing to power greater than you ever dreamed of. It will dawn on you that the real life destined for the awakened few now, and the many in the future is a dazzling dream—a permanent realization that it is a happiness to exist—a serenity and contentment without abatement—a transition from pleasure to pleasure, and from the great to the greater pleasure. You find as you get more and more into the current of the Infinite Mind that exhausting toil is not required of you, but that when you commit yourself in trust to this current and let it bear you where it will, all things needful will come to you.

When you are getting into the right thought current, you may for a time experience more of uneasiness, physical and mental than ever. This is because the new element acting on you makes you more sensitive to the presence of evil. The new is driving the old out. The new thought current searches and detects every little error in your mind before unnoticed, and repels it. This causes a struggle, and mind and body are for a time unpleasantly affected by it. It is like house-cleaning, a process usually involving a good deal of dust and disturbance. The new spirit you call to you is cleaning your spiritual house.

There is no limit to the power of the thought current you can attract to you nor limit to the things that can he done through the individual by it. In the future some people will draw so much of the higher quality of thought to them, that by it they will accomplish what some would call miracles. In this capacity of the human mind for drawing a thought current ever increasing in fineness of quality and power lies the secret of what has been called "magic."

One Way to Cultivate Courage

Courage and presence of mind mean the same thing. Presence of mind implies command of mind. Cowardice and lack of mental control mean about the same thing. Cowardice is rooted in hurry, the habit of hurry or lack of repose. All degrees of success are based on courage—mental or physical. All degrees of failure are based on timidity.

You can cultivate courage and increase it at every minute and hour of the day. You can have the satisfaction of knowing that in everything you do you have accomplished two things—namely, the doing of the thing itself and by the manner of its doing, adding eternally to yourself another atom of the quality of courage. You can do this by the cultivation of deliberation—deliberation of speech, of walk, of writing, of eatlng—deliberation in everything.

There is always a bit of fear where there is a bit of hurry. When you hurry to the train you are in fear that you may be left, and with that comes fear of other possibilities consequent on your being left. When you hurry to the party, to the meeting of a person by appointment, you are in fear of some ill or damage resulting from not being in time.

This habit of thought can, through an unconscious training, grow to such an extent as to pervade a person's mind, at all times and places, and bring on a fear of loss of some kind, when there is absolutely no loss to be sustained. For instance a person may hurry to catch a street car and act and feel as if a great loss would occur did he not get on that particular car, when there may be another close behind, or at most two or three minutes' waiting will bring it. Yet the fear of waiting those three minutes grows to a mountain in size, and is in that person's mind a most disagreeable possibility. Through mere habit a similar condition of hurry may characterize that person's walking, eating, writing—in short, everything he does, and will render it more and more difficult for such person to act with coolness and deliberation.

The quality of mind or emotion underlying all this hurried mental condition and consequent hurried act, is fear. Fear is but another name for lack of power to control our minds, or, in other words, to control the kind of thought we think or put out.

It is this kind of unconscious mental training (which is very common), that begets a permanent condition of mind more and more liable to large and small panics at the least interruption or trivial disappointment. It makes disappointments when none are necessary. It is the ever- opening wedge letting in more and more the thought current of fear. For if you so cultivate fear of one thing you are cultivating and increasing liability to fear in all things. If you allow yourself to sit in fear for half an hour that the carriage may not call for you in time to get to the boat or train, you are much more liable to be seized with a series of little panics at every trivial occurrence or obstacle occurring on that particular journey.

In this way does this habit of mind enter into and is cultivated in the doing of so-called little things. You are writing or sewing, or engaged in the performance of some work which is intensely interesting to you, and in which you do not like to be interrupted. If sewing, you reach for your scissors which have dropped on the floor. You do this in a momentarily impatient mood and with a spasmodic jerky action. Your mind, as the phrase runs, is "on your work." You will not take it off your work while reaching for the scissors. You are trying in mind to go on with your work and reach for the scissors at the same moment. You make the movement of muscles and the action of the body momentarily disagreeable and irksome, because you refuse for the second to put into that act the force which it demands. When unconsciously you refuse to do this, any acts will become irksome and disagreeable, because there is not force enough let on to do the act with ease. It is the endeavour to do it with a weak body. You have the power of throwing your force instantly into any muscle, so making the act easy and pleasant. This capacity for turning on force on any part you will increases through cultivating it. And you can do a great deal more and do it better through this cultivation of deliberation, for deliberation can be as quick as thought, the more the mind is trained in that direction.

If you pick up a pin or tie a shoe-string in a hurry, you do so not only because such act is irksome to you, but because you fear it may deprive you momentarily of some bit of pleasure. There you have again opened your mind to the thought current of fear—fear of losing something.

The cultivation of courage commences in the cultivation of deliberation in so-called little acts like these. Deliberation and courage are as closely allied as fear and hurry. If we do not learn to govern our force properly in the doing of the smallest act we shall find such government far less easy in the doing of all acts.

If we analyze what we fear, we shall find we are in mind trying to deal with too much at once of the thing feared. There is only a relatively small amount to be dealt with now. In any transaction —in the doing of anything there is but one step to be taken at a time. We need to place what force is necessary, and no more on that one step. When that is taken we can take the next.

The more we train our minds so to concentrate on the one step, the more do we increase capacity for sending our force all in one given direction at once. Such force extends, and should be so used in the so-called minutest details of everyday life. In this way deliberation and deliberate action become habitual, and we are in a sense unconscious of making ourselves deliberate, even as after long training in the opposite and wrong direction we are unconscious of putting on the hurried frame of mind.

Timidity is often the result of looking at too many difficulties or terrors at once. In material reality we have to deal with but one at a time. If we are going to what we fear will be a disagreeable interview with a harsh, irascible, over-bearing person, we are apt to go, occupying our minds with the whole interview, setting ourselves down in the very middle of it, and seeing it in mind as necessarily trying or disagreeable. Perhaps we were thinking of it this morning while we were dressing. But it was then our proper business to dress. To dress was a necessary step for the interview and to dress well also. Possibly it occupied our thoughts while eating. But it was then our proper business to eat and get all the pleasure possible from our food. That was another step. The more reposeful our eating, the more vigorous will become our taste, and the more strength will our food give our bodies. Possibly the fear of this interview was on us as we walked to the place appointed for it. But it was then our proper business to walk and get from our walking all the pleasure he could. That was another step. Pleasure is the sure result of placing thought or force on the thing we are doing now, and pain of some sort in both present and future is the certain result of sending thought or force away from the act which needs to be done at this moment.

When we dress, eat, walk or do anything with mind placed on something else, we are making the present act irksome; we are training to make every act irksome and disagreeable; we are making the thing feared a certainty, for what we put out in thought as unpleasant is an actual thing, a reality. And the longer we continue to put it out the more force we add to it, and the more likely is it then to be realized in the physical world.

To bring us what all want and are seeking for, namely-happiness, we need to have perfect control of our mind and thought at all times and places. One most important and necessary means for gaining this, lies in this discipline regarding so-called little or trivial things, just as the discipline and movement of an army commences with the training of the private soldiers' legs and arms. If you hurry and slur over these so-called petty details, you are the easier thrown off your guard or confused at unexpected occurrences, and in life it is the unexpected that is always happening.

We need to keep always our mind present with us. We want it always on the spot ready to use in any direction. Our thought is not on the spot when we tie a shoe-string and think a mile from that shoe-string—when we mend a pencil and dwell in one of tomorrow's cares. It is then away, and if it has for a lifetime been in the habit of so straying from the act in hand to the act afar, it becomes more and more difficult to bring it back to use, and more difficult to use it promptly when it is brought back. Our thought moves from one thing to another with more than electric speed, and we can unconsciously train this quickness to be ever darting from one thing to another until it becomes almost impossible to keep it on one thing for ten consecutive seconds. On the contrary, through cultivation of repose and deliberation in all things we can train ourselves to mass and fasten our thought on anything as long as we please, to throw ourselves into any mood of mind we please, and to throw ourselves at will into sleep or a semi-conscious, dreamy state as restful as sleep. These are very small parts of the possibilities for the human mind. There is no limit to its growth or the increase of its power, and no thing coming within the limits of our imagination but can be accomplished by it. The steps to these attainments are very small, very simple and relatively easy—so simple and easy that some reject them for that reason.

Unquestionably, these powers and many results coming of their exercise were known ages ago to a relative few. But any power or any condition of mind consequent upon it can be made more clear to an English-speaking people, through the use of an English word or form of expression than by terms taken from other languages.

The North American Indian and the Oriental had in cases the power of so dismissing all thought and making their minds in a sense a blank as to become not only insensible to fear, but this mental condition rendered their bodies almost insensible to physical suffering. It was the power of inducing this mental condition which enabled the Indian when taken captive to withstand every device of torture inflicted by his captors, and to sing his death song under the infliction of fire and a slow process of bodily mutilation too horrible for description, and which very few of our race could endure without passing into the frenzy of agony.

The Indian is far more reposeful and deliberate than the majority of our race, in both mental and physical movement. Unconsciously cultivating this repose. and living a life less artificial than ours, he increased his spiritual power, one sure result of which is that command of mind over body which can lessee physical pain, and as an ultimate possibility banish it altogether.

Deliberation of movement, or in plainer English movement of muscle so slow that our mind has time to follow it, gives one time to think in great and small emergencies. But the lack of such training causes unconscious physical action. So confirmed becomes this habit, that the body moves without us aware of it. Awkwardness, lack of address, lack of tact are all due to this lack of command of mind caused by lack of deliberation, or in other words, a trained incapacity for taking time to think or plan the proper thing to do.

The terror-stricken person if the ship seems in sudden danger runs up and down the deck to no purpose, and this physical action is an exact correspondence of the life-long condition of his mind whose thought has been ever so darting from one thing to another, just as the whim seized him.

The more deliberate person whose mind is trained to take time to think and hold or concentrate its thought, holds himself steady, and so gives himself time to see what may be the opportunities for escape. And these two persons would pick up a pin in a very different manner and with very different mental action and method.

To train then for courage is to train for deliberate movement in all things, for that is simply training to mass and hold your force in reserve and let out no more than is needed for the moment.

No quality of mind is more needful to success in all undertakings than courage, and by courage I mean not only courage to act but courage to think. In everyday business, thousands dare not think of taking a step which would involve an outlay of money above the average of their expenditure. They are appalled at mention of so large a sum. They will not, out of pure fright, entertain the idea long enough to familiarize themselves with it. Now if they reversed this mental action, and instead of immediately giving way out of life-long habit to this fright, would take time and allow the thought to rest in their minds instead of driving it out, there would in time come to them ideas concerning ways and means for meeting the additional expense, and thereby making a larger sum of money in the same time it took to make the small sum.

For instance, you say to the women who goes out to wash by the day and has never done anything else. "Mrs. A., why don't you start a laundry? You can make a great deal more money in so doing."

"I start a laundry! Where in the world is the money coming from to start a laundry?" is her reply. Here the woman instead of entertaining your idea gives way immediately to fright concerning what seems to her the immense sum required, and following the same unreasoning, headlong, panicky style of thought, sets up in a moment an opposition to your proposition. She dare think only of working for day's wages as she is called upon by those who hire her. And thousands for this reason dare not think, or find it disagreeable for them to think, of getting into some broader, more responsible and more profitable sphere of business, because they bunch at once all its possible difficulties into a mass, and out of mere habit will look only at that awful and imaginary bunch.

But Mrs. C., the more deliberate washerwoman, hears your proposition and entertains it. In time she says to herself, "Why should I not start a laundry? Other people have and have succeeded." She lives in the idea, talks to one and another about it, and finds out how they started. The longer she keeps in this current of thought the more plainly does she see the ways and means by which other people have "set up for themselves." Finally, the idea so grows upon her, that she takes some step toward that end, and then another and another, and so by degrees drifts into the business.

A person is cool and collected in face of any great danger, because he has the power of holding his mind to the thing to be done on the instant. Cowardice has no such power, and can see in mind not only the source of danger, but a score of possible results which may or may not happen to him. In battle one man may attend to his duty with a vivid and by no means agreeable condition of mind as he sees men struck and mangled all about him. But the force or thought he can bring to bear on the performance of his duty is greater in amount than that coming of the realization of the slaughter around him, and commands and holds his body to his post. The man who runs, or would if he had the chance, cannot fix his mind on anything but the fearful possibilities of the moment.

In the so-called trivial act of picking up a pin, or threading a needle, or opening a door, I do not argue that all one's force or thought should be placed on the act, but only enough to perform the act well while the rest is kept in reserve. It is in substance the same as in picking up a weight, you would not try to expend the force in lifting one pound that you would in lifting fifty pounds. You do expend a great deal more force in the act of picking up a pin when your mind is preoccupied with something else, for you are then trying to do two things or lift two weights at once.

You will remember that anything which is done in mind, expends quite as much force as if done with the body, so that the persons who linger abed in the morning and think with dread of the breakfasts to be cooked, or the rooms to be swept, so far as expenditure of force is concerned, will be doing those acts then and there while lying on their backs.

In expending just force enough to perform any act (a capacity which will gradually grow upon you as you familiarize yourself with this idea and set your desire or demand upon it,) you cultivate and increase continually that desirable state of mind, which in everyday language is known as "having your wits about you." That means, in other words, always having, no matter what you are doing, your mental eyes open in every direction, and while outwardly you seem all intent and occupied in the one act, your mind or spirit like a vigilant sentinel is continually on the look-out, so as to give you notice in the fractional part of an instant of all that is going on about you, and also to direct you how to meet the event whatever it may be. This is not only the characteristic of courage, but of tact and address. It was this electric vigilance and mind watchfulness that gave an American officer during the Revolution, who, in the confusion of battle, suddenly found himself in front of a British regiment, the deliberation to ask, "What troops are these?" "The Royal Scots," was the reply. " Royal Scots remain as you are," was his answer, and he rode off to his own lines. That man had a mind trained to give him time to think.

On one occasion, Mrs. Farren, the celebrated English actress, discovered where her part required her to hem a handkerchief that the property man had forgotten to lay out the handkerchief needle, thread, etc. Without a moment's hesitation she sat down and imitated so naturally the motion and manner of a lady in sewing that most of her audience never suspected the omission. That act involved self possession, coolness, deliberation, presence of mind, courage. Do not all these terms imply a similar state of mind? A woman habitually hurried and flurried could not have done this, and I believe that when Mrs. Farren saw proper to pick up a pin, she did so in a much more deliberate manner than would the habitually hurried, flurried man or woman.

Cultivate deliberate act and movement in all things, and you lay more and more the solid foundation for courage, either moral or physical. But deliberate act does not always imply slowness. Just as thought moves with electric rapidity, so may it move the body when occasion requires, but the thought must be clearly planned, seen and outlined in mind before it is allowed to act on the body. It is so seen or planned, and so acts to use the muscles in the rapid thrust and parry of the skilled fencer, and similarly with the professional danseuse, in fact in all superior accomplishments, be they of painter, musician or other artist. These, however, in many cases, are but partial controls of mind. Outside of his art, the artist may have little mental control or deliberation, and as a result be "nervous" vacillating, easily disturbed, whimsical and timid. The mind is our garrison to be armed at all points and disciplined to meet any emergency.

We deal with the making (or self-making) of whole men and women, whose minds are not cultivated all in one direction and neglected everywhere else. It is far better in the end to be growing symmetrically and to be finished so far as we have grown "all around," than to have our power all concentrated on one talent or capacity, and becoming what the world calls a "Genius." The inside history of Genius is often a sad one, and shows that it brought little happiness to its possessor.

Scores and hundreds of the little acts of everyday life, such as picking dropped articles from the floor, opening and shutting drawers, laying or reaching for articles on the toilet table, and attending to minor details of dress, are done unconsciously in this hurried condition of mind, especially when some more important object engages our attention. We snatch, we clutch, we drive recklessly about in the doing of these things, and we weaken our bodies and become tired out, and finally "panicky," and easily frightened through this mental habit, for fear and cowardice slip in far more easily when the body is weak.

This habit cannot be changed in a day or a year when it has pervaded a lifetime. Neither can the ills, mental and physical, resulting from such habit, be cured immediately. There can be only gradual growth away from them.

If in reading this you feel convinced that there is "something in it," and feel also a conviction that some portion of it suits your own case, your cure has then commenced. Real conviction, the conviction that comes from within, never leaves one or stops working to get us out of the evil way and put us in the good one. It may seem buried and forgotten for seasons, and our erroneous habits may seem growing stronger than ever. That is not so. But as convictions take root we are seeing our errors more and more clearly. We forget that at one time we were blind and did not see them at all.

If this book brings to you a conviction of a long established error it is not I individually who bring or convince. It is only that I put out more or less of a truth, which takes hold of you and the chord of truth in you senses it. If I apply the torch to the gas-jet and light it, it does not follow that I make either the fire or the gas. I am only a means or agent for lighting that gas. No man makes or invents a truth. Truth is as general and widely spread and belongs to every individual as much as the air we breathe, and there is pleasure enough in being its torch-bearer without presuming to claim the power of its Creator.

Above all demand more and more courage of the Supreme Power.

Look Forward!

The tendency with many people after they are a little "advanced in years" is to look backward and with regret. The "looking" should be the other way—forward. If you want to go backward in every sense, mental and physical, keep on cultivating the mood of living regretfully in your past life.

It is one chief characteristic of the material mind to hold tenaciously to the past. It likes to recall the past and mourn over it. The material mind has a never-ending series of solemn amusement, in recalling past joys, and feeling sad because they are never to come again.

But the real self, the spirit, cares relatively little for its past. it courts change. II expects to be a different individual in thought a year hence from that it is today. It is willing a thousand years hence to forget who or what it is today, for it knows that this intense desire to remember itself for what it has been retards its advance toward greater power and greater pleasure. What care you for what you were a thousand or five thousand years ago? Yet then you were something, and something far less than what you are today. You are curious you may answer to know what you were. Yes, but is curiosity worth gratifying, if for such gratification you must pay the price of dragging after you a hundred corpses of your dead selves. Those selves, those existences, have done their work for you. In doing that work they brought you possibly more pain than pleasure. Do you want ever to bear with you the memory and burden of that pain? Especially when such burden brings more pain and deprives you of pleasure. It is like the bird that should insist on carrying with it always the shell from which it was hatched. If you have a sad remembrance fling it off. If you can't fling it off, demand of the Supreme Power aid to help you do so, and such aid will come. If you want to grow old, feeble, gray and withered, go at once and live in your past, and regret your youth. Go and to revisit places and houses where you lived twenty, thirty, forty years ago; call back the dead; mourn over them; live in remembrance over the joys you had there, and say they are gone and fled and will never come again.

In so doing you are fastening dead selves all over you. If we came into another physical life with the memory of the last one, we should come into the world physically as miniature, decrepit, grizzled old men and women. Youth physically is fresh and blooming, because it packs no past sad material remembrances with it. A girl is beautiful because her spirit has flung off the past and sad remembrance of its previous life, and has therefore a chance for a period to assert itself. A woman commences to "age" then she commences to load up with regrets over a past but twenty years gone.

Your spirit demands for the body it uses grace, agility of movement and personal beauty, for it is made in the "image of God," and the infinite mind and life, beauty, grace and agility are the characteristics of that mind. In that phase of existence we called childhood and youth, the spirit has the chance to assert its desire for beauty and agility, because it has not as yet loaded up with false beliefs and regrets.

The liveliness, sprightliness and untiring playfulness of the boy or girl of ten or twelve, is due to the gladness of spirit relieved of the burden that is carried in a past existence. That burden was one of thoughts unprofitable to carry. You would physically have the agility you had at fifteen could you fling off the burden of sad remembrance and belief in error that you have been loading up with these twenty or thirty years past.

You can commence the unloading process now, by resolving, with the aid of the Supreme Power, to fling off the remembrance of everything in the past that has annoyed you, everything you regret, everything you have mourned over.

God never mourns or regrets. You as a spirit are made in His image. God it eternal life, joy and serenity. The more of these characteristics you reflect the nearer are you to the Infinite Spirit of Good.

Have you buried your dearest on earth? You do them no good by your sad thoughts concerning them. You place bar twixt their spirit and yours in thinking of them as "lost." You may in so doing not only increase and encourage in them a sad mental condition, but bring their gloomy mental condition on yourself, as many do in grieving. The greatest good we can do them is to think of them as alive like ourselves, and to fling their graves, tombstones, coffins, shrouds and ghastliness out of our minds. If we cannot do so of ourselves let us demand help of the Supreme Power to do it. We often make those who have lost their bodies feel dead when we think of them as such. If we do this they will throw back their thoughts of deadness on us.

Keep out of graveyards. It may seem to some that I am cold and unfeeling to say thus, but the truth, as it presents itself to me, says that the graveyard where your loved ones do not lie, is spiritually a most unhealthy place to visit. They are full of the thought of regret, death and decay. When you visit them you incorporate such thought into yourself. It is hostile and killing to youth, vigour, elasticity, cheerfulness and life.

Our graveyards are full of lies, We place a stone over the cast-off body of a friend. We place on that stone the word "died." That is not true. Your friend is not dead. It is only the body he used that lies there. But that grave is planted in your memory, and your friend in your mind lies in it. Do what we will, try to believe what we may of the eternal prolongation of life and the impossibility of anything like death in the universe, we cannot help making for ourselves when we think of that grave or revisit it, an image of that friend as dead and decaying in his or her coffin. This image we fasten in our minds, and in so doing we fasten on ourselves the thought of gloom, death and decay. The thoughts of decay and death are things and forces. When we keep them so much in mind we add elements of decay to the body.

We need as much as possible to fasten our thought on life and increasing life—life greater in its activity than any we have ever realized. That is not gained by looking backward. Look forward.

Every regret, every mournful thought, takes so much out of your life. It is force used to pile on more misery. It is force used to strengthen the habit of regretting. It is force used to make the mind colour everything with a tinge of sadness, and the longer you use force in this way the darker will grow the tinge.

Also, when we are ever going back in memory to the past and living in it in preference to the present we are bringing back on ourselves the old moods of mind and mental conditions belonging to that past. This feeling constantly indulged in will bring on some form of physical ailment. The ailment belongs to a condition of mind which we should be done with forever. If we are looking forward we shall shake it off and be better in health than ever. If the predominant mood of our minds is that of looking backward, the ultimate result will be serious to the body.

In the world's business your active, enterprising pushing man of affairs spends little time in sad reminiscence. If he did his business would suffer. His thought is forward. That thought is the real force which pushes his business forward. If he spent it in " sad memories" of the past his business would go backward. He works his success (so far as he does really succeed) by this spiritual law, though he may not know it.

You may be saying: "I have failed in life and shall always be a failure." That is because you are ever leaking back, living in your failure and thereby bringing to you more failure. Reverse this attitude of mind; work it the other way and live in future success.

Why do you say: " I am always sick?" Because you are looking back, living in your past ailments and thereby bringing more on you.

I have heard the expression used: " When the earth was young." As if this planet was now in its dotage and going to decay! In the sense of freshness, increase of life, refinement and purity in every form of life, be that of man, animal, vegetable, and farther on, this earth never was so young as it is today. Youth is life, growing and increasing in beauty and power. It is not the cruder commencement of life.

The so-called "barren rock" contains elements which will help to form the future tree and flower. Is that part of the rock which enters into tree and flower increasing or decreasing in life? It changes only into a higher and more beautiful expression of life. So do we from age to age. The rock crumbles that it may live in this higher form. The old mind must crumble and pass away to give place to the new, and make of us the newer spiritual being. As the old mind crumbles so will the old body, for the spiritual change must be accompanied by the physical change. But if you live in the understanding and spirit of this law you need not lose a physical body, but have one ever changing for the better. As you live in spiritual belief, as the old life goes out the new comes in.

Nothing in Nature—nothing in the Universe is at a standstill. Nothing goes backward. A gigantic incomprehensible Force and Wisdom moves all things forward toward greater and higher powers and possibilities. You are included in and are a part of this Force. There is of you in embryo the power of preventing the physical body your spirit uses from decaying, and the power also of using it in ways which even the fiction of today would discard as too wild for the pages of the novel.

For your spirit youth and ever growing youth is an eternal. heritage. If your body has "aged" that is no sign that your spirit has "aged." The spirit cannot grow old in the material sense, anymore than the sunlight can grow old. If your body has "aged" it is because that body has become the material likeness and expression of a false self or "shell" which has formed on your spirit. That false self is made up of thoughts prevalent around from an early physical age and those thoughts are untrue thoughts. A large proportion of that thought is regret. Regret is an inverted force—a turning of the mind to look backward when its natural and healthy state is to look forward, and live in the joys that are certain to come when we do look forward.

In the new life to come to our race, when we have learned to be ever looking forward to the greater joys to come and cease to look backward and drag the dead past with us, men and women are to have bodies far more beautiful and graceful than those of today.

Because their bodies will image or reflect their thoughts, and their thoughts will ever be fixed on what is beautiful and symmetrical. They will know that what is to come and what is in store for them out of the richness of the Infinite mind must exceed anything they have realized in the past.

Today with the great majority of people their attitude of mind is directly the reverse. Owing to the little trust that they have in that Power the theologian calls "God," they are ever in their minds saying: "There are no joys to come for us like our past joys. Our youth has fled. Our future on earth is tame and dull. It is as dust and ashes."

The truth that life does not end with the death of the body makes slow progress in fixing itself firmly in our minds. The kind of life a man may be living here at seventy does not end in the grave. It continues straight on.

The "old man," as we call him here, wakes up in the other side of life after losing his body an old man still. If he is one of those old men who have "outlived their day and generation," who live in their physical past and look back on it with regret—who have become "too old to learn," and think they have got through with it all, he will be just such an old man in the world of spirit. There is no sudden transformation into youth on the death of a worn-out decrepit body. As the tree falls so does it lie for a period, even in the hereafter.

But in this state he cannot stay forever. He must grow not in age but youth. To do this it is necessary not only that he should leave the old body but the old material mind that made that body. His spirit throws off that mind when he gains a new body (or is reincarnated), and he throws it off because he loses the recollection of all past sad memories and regrets.

The man should in mind be always the boy, the woman, the girl. You can as man or woman be always boy or girl in spirit without being silly or losing real dignity. You can have all the playfulness of youth with the wisdom of maturity. To have a clear powerful mind you need not be an owl.

There may be for a period a certain use for us in going back to our more recent past lives, and for a time living in them. Sometimes we are pushed back temporarily into some old condition of mind, some old experience in order to make us more alive than ever to the rags and tatters of errors in belief still clinging to us.

This may come of revisiting places and people from whom we have long been separated. For a time during such visit old associations, the moods connected with them and possibly old habits we thought long since cast off, resume their sway. We may become for a time absorbed and swallowed up in the old life. We resume temporarily an old mind or mental condition that was formerly our permanent one in that place or association.

But after a little the new mind, the new self into which we have grown during the long absence, antagonizes the old. It feels aversion and disgust for the narrow life, the false beliefs and the dull, monotonous purposeless lives about it. It (the spirit) refuses to have anything to do with the old.

Then comes a conflict between our two minds, the old and the new, which may result in temporary physical sickness. Our old life or self rises as it were out of its grave and tries to fasten itself on the new and even rule the new. The new self rejects the corpse with horror. But through thus seeing the corpse, it sees also fragments of the old self which, unperceived have all along been adhering to the new. We do not get rid of error in belief all at once, and often unconsciously retain shreds of such belief when we imagine ourselves entirely rid of them. These shreds are the remains of old thoughts and former mental conditions. Your new mind so awakened arises and pushes off what it finds left on it of the old. This pushing off is accompanied by physical disturbance, because your spirit puts all its force in rejecting these fragments of the former self, as you might put all your physical strength in pushing off a snake.

Our old errors in belief must be so pushed off before the new thoughts, which come in as the old go out, can have full sway. If your spirit was contentedly and blindly carrying any scorpion of false belief, you would tumble into the pit eventually as so many are now doing. When you live several years in any certain house or town or locality, you make a spiritual self belonging to that locality. Every house, tree, road or other object you have long been in the habit of seeing there, has a part of that self in thought attached to it. Every person who knows you there has in his or her mind the self you make there, and puts that self out then they meet you or talk of you.

If you had years before in that place, the reputation of being weak, or vacillating, or impractical, or intemperate, and you returned to the people who knew you as such, although you may have changed for the better, you are very liable in their thought and recollection of you to have this old self pushed back on you, and as a result, you may for a period feel much like your former self.

You return to such place after a long absence. You have during that absence changed radically in belief. You bring with you a different mind. You are in reality a different person. But the old "you," the old self of former years will rise from every familiar object to meet you. It will come out of houses formerly inhabited by your friends, though now tenanted by strangers; you will find it in the village church, the old schoolhouse, the very rails and fence posts familiar to you long years before. More than all it will come out of the recollection of people who only knew you for what you were, say twenty years before; every such person strengthens with you this image of your former self. You talk with them on the plane of that previous life or self. For the time being you ignore yourself as it now thinks and believes; you put aside your newer self, not wishing to obtrude on your friends opinions, which to them may be unpleasant, or seem wild and visionary; you meet perhaps twenty-five or thirty people who know you only as your former self, and with all these you act out the old self, and repress the new, This for a time makes the old dead self very strong, but you cannot keep this up; you cannot warm the old corpse of yourself into life. If you try to—if you try to be and live your former self, you will become depressed mentally, and very likely sick physically; you may find yourself going into moods of mind peculiar to your former life which you thought had gone forever; you may find yourself beset with physical ailment also peculiar to that period from which you had not suffered for years. Such ailments are not real. They are but the thoughts and wrong beliefs which your old "you" is trying to fasten on you.

I visited recently a place from which I had been absent twenty-five years. I had spent there a portion of my physical youth, and had lived there with a mind or belief very different from that which I entertain now.

I returned to find the place dead in more senses than one. The majority of my old acquaintances had passed away. Their remains lay in the graveyards. But I realized this deadness still more among my contemporaries who were said to be living. They had lost the spur and activity of their youthful ambition. They had resigned themselves to "growing old." They lived mostly in the past, talked of the past "good old times," and compared the present and future unfavourably with the past. They were in mind about where I left them twenty-five years before, and about where I was in mind when I did leave them.

Drawn temporarily into their current of thought "for old acquaintance sake," I talked with them of the past, and for some days lived in it. At every turn I met something animate or inanimate to bring back my past life to me.

Then I went to the graveyards, and in thought renewed acquaintance with those whose remains lay there. So I lived for days unconscious, that in these moods of sad reminiscence I was drawing to me elements of decay sadness.

First becoming very much depressed, I was next taken strangely sick, and became so weak I could hardly stand. I was continually in a nervous tremor and full of vague fears.

Why was this? Because in going back into my past life I had drawn on me my old mental conditions—my old mind—my own self of that period. But since that time I had grown a new mind—a new self, which thought and believed very differently from the old.

The new self into which I had grown since leaving that locality would not accept the old. It shook it off. It was the shaking off process that caused me the physical disturbance. There was a conflict between these two forces, one trying to get in, the other to keep it out. My body was the battle-ground between the two. No battle-ground is a serene place to live on when the battle is going on.

It was necessary in this case that I should look backward and live backward for a season to show me more clearly the evil of doing so. For no lesson can be really learned without an experience. It was not merely the evil of living backward in that particular locality that I came to see clearly. I saw also for the first time, where I had unconsciously been living in the past, and living backward in numberless ways and thereby unconsciously, using up force, which would have pushed me forward in every sense.

I understood, also, after passing through this process, why weeks before visiting that place I had felt depressed, and experienced also a return of certain moods of mind I had not felt for years. It was because my spirit was already in that place and working through this change. The culminating point was reached when my material self touched that locality.

All changes are wrought out in spirit often before our material senses are in the least aware of them. Let no one imagine that because I write of these Spiritual Laws that I am able to live fully in accordance with them. I am not above error or mistake. I tumble into pits occasionally, get off the main track—and get on again.

Power comes of looking forward with hope—of expecting and demanding the better things to come. That is the law of the Infinite Mind, and when we follow it we live in that mind.

Nature buries its dead as quickly as possible and gets them out of sight. It is better, however, to say that Nature changes what it has no further use for into other terms of life. The live tree produces the new leaf with each return of spring. It will have nothing to do with its dead ones. It treasures up no withered rose leaves to bring back sad remembrance. When the tree itself ceases to produce leaf and blossom, it is changed into another form and enters into other forms of vegetation.

I do not mean to imply that we should try to banish all past remembrance. Banish only the sad part. Live as much as you please in whatever of your past that has given you healthy enjoyment. There are remembrances of woodland scenes, of fields of waving rain. of blue skies and white-capped curling billows, and many another of Nature's expressions as connected with your individual life, that can be recalled with pleasure and profit. These are not of the decaying past. These are full of life, freshness and beauty, and are of today.

But if with these any shade of sadness steals in, reject it instantly. Refuse to accept it. It is not a part of the cheerful life-giving remembrance. It is the cloud which if you give it the least chance will overshadow the whole and turn it all to gloom.

The science of happiness lies in controlling our thought and getting thought from sources of healthy life.

When your mind is diverted from possibly the long habit of thinking and living in the gloomy side of things and admitting gloomy thought, you will find to your surprise that the very place the sight of which gave you pain will give you pleasure, because you have banished a certain unhealthy mental condition, into which you before allowed yourself to drift. You can then revisit the localities connected with your past, remember and live only in the bright and lively portion of that past, and reject all thought about "sad changes," and "those who have passed away, never to return, etc." I have proven this to myself.

Is there any use or sense in admitting things to have access to you which only pain and injure you? Does God commend any self-destroying, suicidal act? Grief does nothing but destroy the body.

God in the Trees: Or, The Infinite Mind in Nature

You are fortunate if you love trees, and especially the wild ones growing where the Great Creative Force placed them, and independent of man's care. For all things we call "wild" or "natural" are nearer the Infinite Mind than those which have been enslaved, artificialized and hampered by man. Being nearer the Infinite they have in them the more perfect Infinite Force and Thought That is why when you are in the midst of what is wild and natural—in the forest or mountains, where every trace of man's works is left behind you feel an indescribable exhilaration and freedom that you do not realize elsewhere.

You breathe an element ever being thrown off by the trees, the rocks, the birds and animals and by every expression of the Infinite Mind about you. It is healthfully exhilarating. It is something more than air. It is the Infinite Force and Mind as expressed by all these natural things, which is acting on you. You cannot get this force in the town, nor even in the carefully cultivated garden. For there the plants and trees have too much of man's lesser mind in them—the mind which believes that it can improve the universe. Man is inclined to think that the Infinite made this world in the rough, and then left it altogether for him to improve,

Are we really doing this in destroying the native forests, as well as the birds and animals, which once dwelt in them? Are our rivers, many of them laden with the filth of sewage and factory, and our ever expanding cities and towns, covering miles with piles of brick and mortar, their inhabitants crammed into the smallest living quarters, honeycombed with sewers below, and resounding with rattle and danger above·—are these really "improvements" on the Divine and natural order of things?

You are fortunate when you grow to a live, tender, earnest love for the wild trees, animals and birds, and recognize then all as coming from and built of the same mind and spirit as your own, and able also to give you something very valuable in return for the love you give them. The wild tree is not irresponsive or regardless of a love like that. Such love is not a myth or mere sentiment. It is a literal element and force going from you to the tree. It is felt by the spirit of the tree. You represent a part and belonging of the Infinite Mind. The tree represents another part and belonging of the Infinite Mind. It has its share of life, thought and intelligence. You have a far greater share, which is to be greater still—and then still greater.

Love is an element which though physically unseen is as real as air or water. It is an acting, living, moving force, and in that far greater world of life all around us, of which physical sense is unaware, it moves in waves and currents like those of the ocean.

There is a sense in the tree which feels your love and responds to it. It does not respond or show its pleasure in our way or in any way we can now understand. Its way of so doing is the way or the Infinite Mind of which it is a part. The ways of God are unsearchable and past finding out. They are not for us to fathom. They are for us only to find out and live out, in so far as they make us happier. There is for all in time a serenity and "peace of mind which passeth all understanding;" but this peace cannot be put through a chemical analysis or the operation of the dissecting room.

As the Great Spirit has made all things, is not that All Pervading Mind and wisdom in all things? If then we love the trees, the rocks and all things as the Infinite made them, shall they not in response to our love give us each of their peculiar thought and wisdom? Shall we not draw nearer to God through a love for these expressions of God in the rocks and trees, birds and animals?

Do we expect to find God, realize him more every day, appreciate the mighty and Immeasurable Mind more every day, and get more and more of His Power in us every day only by dwelling on the word of three letters, G-o-d?

You laugh, perhaps, at the idea of a tree having a mind—a tree that thinks. But the tree has an organization like your own in many respects. It has for blood its sap. It has a circulation. It has for skin its bark. It has for lungs its leaves. It must have its food. It draws nourishment from soil, air and sun. It adapts itself to circumstances. The oak growing in exposed situations roots itself more firmly in the soil to withstand the tempest. The pines growing thickly together take little root, for they depend on numbers to break the wind's force. The sensitive plant recoils at the approach of man's hand; many wild plants, like Indians, will not grow or thrive in artificial conditions.

Yet with all these physical resemblances to your own body, you deny the tree or plant such share of mind as the Infinite gives it? No, not that. The tree is a part of the Infinite Mind, even as you are. It is one of the All Pervading Mind's myriads of thoughts. We see only such part or form of that thought as is expressed in trunk, root, branch and leaf, even as with ourselves we see only our physical bodies. We do not see our spiritual part. Nor do we see in the tree its spiritual part.

The tree is then literally one of God's thoughts. That thought is worth our study. It contains some wisdom we have not yet got hold of. We want that wisdom. We want to make it a part of ourselves. We want it, because real wisdom or truth brings us power. We want power to give us better bodies, sounder bodies, healthier bodies. We want entire freedom from sickness. We want lighter hearts and happier minds. We want a new life and a new pleasure in living for each day. We want our bodies to grow lighter, not heavier with advancing years. We want a religion which will give us certainty instead of hopes and theories. We want a Deity it is simply impossible to doubt. We want to feel the Infinite Mind in every atom of our beings. We want with each day to feel a new pleasure in living and, commencing where we left off yesterday, to find something new in what we might have thought to be "old" and worn out yesterday. When we come into the domain of the Infinite Mind and are ever drawing more of that mind to us and making it a part of us, nothing can seem "flat, stale and unprofitable."

We want powers now denied the mortal. We want to be lifted above the cumbrousness of the mortal body—above the pains of the mortal body—above the death of the mortal body.

Can the trees give us all this? They can help very much so to do when we get into their spirit; when we recognize and realize more and more the reality of that part of the Infinite which they express, and when we can cease to look on them as inanimate creatures.

If you can look on trees as fit only for lumber and firewood you get very little life from them. They feel then toward you as you would feel towards a person who regarded you as a thing without mind or sense and fit only to he sawed into lumber or firewood.

When we come really to love God or the Infinite Spirit of Good, we shall love every part of God. A tree is a part of God. When we come to send out our love to it, it will send its love back, and that love—that literal mind and element coming from the tree to us will enter our beings, add itself to them and give us its knowledge and power. It will tell us that the mind and force it represents of the Infinite has far better uses for man than to be turned into fuel or lumber. Their love will tell us that the forests piercing the air as they do with their billions of branches, twigs and leaves, are literal conductors for a literal element which they bring to the earth. This element is life giving to man, in proportion to his capacity for receiving it.

The nearer we are to a conception of the Infinite Mind—the clearer is it seen by us that this mind pervades all things—the closer we feel our relationship to the tree, bird or animal as a fellow creature, the more can we absorb of the vitalizing element given out by all these expressions of mind. The person who looks on trees as fit only for fuel and lumber, can get but little of this element, which to the finer mind is an elixir of life.

The mind which sees in tree, bird, animal, fish or insect only a thing lacking intelligence and fit only to destroy or enslave for amusement, repels from all of these a spirit or element, which, if recognized, would be received or absorbed, and, if absorbed, would bring a new life and power to mind and body.

We get the element of love only in proportion as we have it in us. We can only draw this element from the Supreme Power. We draw it in proportion as we admire every expression of the Infinite, be that expression tree, or shrub, or insect, or bird, or other form of the Natural, We cannot destroy or mutilate what we realty love. The more of these things we really love, the more of their element of love flows to us. That element is for us life as real Is the tree itself. The more of that life we are receiving and absorbing, the more shall we realize a power in life, which can only be expressed as miraculous.

Destroy the forests, and you lessen temporarily the quantity of this element given out by them. Replace the wild tree by exotics or cultivated varieties, and such element is adulterated, and the vigour it can give is lessened. Cover the whole earth with cities, towns, villages and cultivated fields, and we interfere with a supply of life-giving element which the forests in their natural state only can furnish. Keep ourselves dead to the recognition of the tree as a part of the Infinite Spirit, and we are dead and unable to absorb of the Infinite Spirit working in and through the tree.

The trees are always giving out an element of life as necessary to man as the air he breathes. Man's works, as soon as finished, are giving out dust and decay. In our great cities we take in dust with every breath. Nothing in this Universe is still or in absolute rest. Our miles of stone, brick and mortar are ever in movement, slowly and imperceptibly grinding to an impalpable dust. Cloth, leather, iron, and every material worn and used by man is ever wearing into dust. Look at the dust which in a single day accumulates in your room, on shelf and table, or fine garment, even when its windows are not opened. A gigantic ever-moving force is at work there taking everything to pieces in it. Let a sunbeam enter through a shutter's crack and see the innumerable motes floating in it. Think of the myriads of these, too minute to rank even as atoms that you cannot see.

All this is second-hand element which is breathed and absorbed into both body and spirit. But trees and all natural things send out element full of life.

Our bodies also are ever throwing off through the skin matter they can no longer use. In the great city thousands on thousands of bodies are throwing out disused element too fine to rank even as dust. It is thrown off by sick bodies, and many are sick on their feet. This we breathe. We breathe each other over and over again.

This unseen cloud of matter pervading crowded cities is not life sustaining. It has in it a certain life as all things have life, but it is not fit for man's growing life.

When we get eternal life, health and unalloyed happiness, the attitude of our minds will be entirely changed toward tree, bird, animal, and everything in Nature. We shall see that when we really love all these expressions of the Infinite Mind, tree, plant, bird and animal, and leave them entirely alone, they will send out to us in love their part and quality of the Infinite. It will flow to us a new life, and the source of a life of far greater power and happiness than the present one.

"But how shall we live," one asks," unless we cut down the tree for fuel and lumber, slay bird and beast for food?" Do you think there is no other life or way of life than the one we now live? Do you think in the exalted and refined mental condition we call "Heaven" that there will be killing of animals, mutilation of trees and destruction of any material expression of the Supreme Wisdom? Do you think we can grow into that higher and happier state of mind without knowledge of the laws by which only it can be attained? As well expect to sail a ship around the world without knowledge of seamanship or navigation. We are not to drift into Heaven in the way a cask rolls down hill.

We cannot cease immediately from the enslavement or slaughter of tree, bird or animal, nor from the eating of animal food. So long as the body craves and relishes such food, it should have it. When the body is changed by our spirit and belief to finer elements, the stomach and palate will reject meat of every description. It will not abide the taste or smell of slaughtered creatures. When the spirit settles these matters it does so definitely and forever. Man's error in the past has often been that of endeavouring to spiritualize or change himself of his own individual will into higher and finer conditions. To this end he has enforced on himself and others fasts and penances, and abstinence from pleasures which his nature craved. He has never by such methods saved himself from sickness, decay and physical death. He has never by this method regenerated or renewed his body. He has lost his body eventually even as the glutton and drunkard lost theirs.

The ascetic has not trusted in the Supreme to raise him higher in the scale of being, but in himself and his own endeavour. This is one of the greatest sins, because it cuts such a person off temporarily from the Supreme and the life, the Supreme will send when trusted. There is no way out of any sin, any excess, any injurious habit, but through an entire dependence on the Supreme Power to take away the gnawing, the craving, the desire peculiar to that habit. Otherwise the man may seem reformed outwardly. He is never reformed inwardly. Repression is not reform.

The bigot of every age and creed has been the person thinking he could of himself make himself an angel. Such belief makes the man stand still in his tracks. The Supreme is always saying, "Come to me. Demand of me. Find me in all created things and then I shall be ever sending you new thoughts, new things, new ideas, new element which shall change your tastes, your appetites—which shall gradually take away grossness, eliminate gradually fierce, insatiate, lawless desire and hurricane of passion, and bring to you pleasures you cannot now realize."

We shall see more and more clearly in time that when we get the higher, finer and more enduring life (to which all must grow), we shall have the greatest possible inducement to give the trees, plants, birds, animals and all other expressions of the Infinite their lives and their fullest liberty. We shall be compelled to love them. What we really love we cannot abuse, kill or enslave.

We cage a bird for our own pleasure. We do not cage the bird for its pleasure. That is not the highest love for the bird.

The highest love for all things is for us a literal source of life. The more things in the world of Nature to which we can give the higher love, the more of their natural love and life shall we get in return. So, as we grow, refine and increase this power of recognizing and loving the bird, the animal, the insect or, in other words, the Infinite in all things, we shall receive a love, a renewed life, strength, vigour, cheer and inspiration from not only these, but the falling snow-flake, the driving rain, the cloud, the sea, the mountain. And this will not be a mere sentiment, but a great means for recuperating and strengthening the body, for this strengthens the spirit with a strength which comes to stay, and what strengthens the spirit must strengthen the body.

We cannot make of ourselves this capacity for so loving and drawing strength from all things. It is our belonging, but must be demanded of the Supreme Power.

It is natural to ask, "But why did not the Supreme Power implant at first this higher love in us? Why has that power so long permitted man to go on slaughtering and marring nature? Why are tempests and earthquakes and wars and so much in the forces of Nature and the forces of man allowed to go on and bring so much catastrophe and misery?"

We do not undertake to answer for the Infinite Wisdom. It is enough for us to know that there is a road leading away from all we call evil. It is enough for us to know that the time is to come when as new beings with changed minds we shall forget absolutely that such evils ever existed. We shall see in the forces of Nature, be they fire or tempest, or aught else, only what is good and what can bring us happiness. We are not always to be of the material which can be injured by fire or tempest. The fiery furnace did not affect the three jewish children who walked through it, nor was the tempest of any inconvenience to the Christ of Judea when he walked on the waters. What history has shown to be possible for some is possible for all.

Communion with Nature is something far above a sentiment. It is a literal joining with the Infinite Being. The element received in such joining and acting on mind and body, is as real as anything we see or feel.

The ability so to join ourselves with God through His expressions in the cloud, the tree, the mountain and sea, the bird and animal, is not possessed by all in equal degree. Some are miserable when alone in the forest, plain or mountain. These are literally out of their element or current of thought. They can live with comfort only in the bustle of the town or the chatter of the household. They can find life only in artificial surroundings. Their spirits are covered with a parasitical growth of artificiality. This cuts them off from any sense of God's expressions in the solitude of Nature. So cut off they feel lonesome in the woods. Nature seems wild, savage and gloomy to them.

Whoever can retire for periods to Nature's solitudes and enjoy that solitude, feeling no solitude at all, but a joyous sense of exhilaration, will return among men with more power and new power. For he or she has literally "walked with God " or the Infinite Spirit of Good. The seer, the prophet, the miracle workers of the Biblical history so gained their power. The Christ of Judea retired to the mountains to be reinforced by the Infinite. The Oriental and the Indian, through whom superior powers have been expressed, loved Nature's solitudes. They could live in them with pleasure. They could muse by rock or rivulet or the ocean for hours, almost unconscious of immediate surroundings, because their spirits had strayed far from their bodies, and were dreamily absorbing new ideas of the Infinite. You will rarely find a person who as ruler, soldier, inventor, discoverer, poet or writer left his impress on the race, but loved communion where God is most readily found. There inspiration is born. The poet cannot sing of the city laid out at right angles, with sewer beneath and elevated road above, as he can of the rugged mountain wrapped "like Jura in her misty shroud."

We cannot train ourselves to this capacity for enjoyment of the natural things of earth or for drawing strength from them. To assume a virtue when we have it not, is to be forced, "gushy " and sentimentally silly. But when we demand persistently of the Infinite the new mind, which can find and feel God in the forest or on the sea, in the storm and tempest, and feel not only safety, but absorb power and strength, when Nature's forces seem in their most angry mood, that mind with that capacity will gradually take place of the old one, and with the "new mind" all things will become new."

Some Laws of Health and Beauty

Your thoughts shape your face, and give it its peculiar expression. Your thoughts determine the attitude, carriage, and shape of your whole body.

The law for beauty and the law for perfect health is the same. Both depend entirely on the state of a your mind; or, in other words, on the kind of thoughts you most put out and receive.

Ugliness of expression comes of unconscious transgressions of a law, be the ugliness in the young or the old. Any form of decay in a human body, any form of weakness, anything in the personal appearance of a man or woman which makes them repulsive to you, is because their prevailing mood of mind has made them so.

Nature plants in us what some call "instinct," what we call the higher reason, because it comes of the exercise of a finer set of senses than our outer or physical senses, to dislike everything that is repulsive or deformed, or that shows signs of decay. That is the inborn tendency in human nature to shun the imperfect, and seek and like the relatively perfect. Your higher reason is right in disliking wrinkles or decrepitude, or any form or sign of the body's decay, for the same reason you are right in disliking a soiled or torn garment. Your body is the actual clothing, as well as the instrument used by your mind or spirit. It is the same instinct, or higher reason making you like a well-formed and beautiful body, that makes you like a new and tasteful suit of clothes.

You and generations before you, age after age, have been told it was an inevitable necessity, that it was the law and in the order of nature for all times and all ages, that after a certain period in life your body must wither and become unattractive, and that even your minds must fail with increasing years. You have been told that your mind had no power to repair and recuperate your body—to make it over again, and make it newer and fresher continually.

It is no more in the inevitable order of Nature, that human bodies should decay as peoples' bodies have decayed in the past, than that man should travel only by stage-coach as he did sixty years ago; or that messages could be sent only by letter as they were fifty years ago, before the use of the electric telegraph; or that your portraits could be taken only by the painter's brush as they were half a century ago, before the discovery that the sun could imprint an image of yourself, an actual part of yourself, on a sensitive surface prepared for it.

It is the impertinence of a dense ignorance for any of us to say what is in or what is to be in the order of nature. It is a stupid blunder to look back at the little we know of the past, and say that it is the unerring index finger telling us what is to be in the future.

If this planet has been what geology teaches it has been,—a planet fuller of coarser, cruder, and more violent forces than now; abounding in forms of coarser vegetable, animal, and even human life and organization than now; of which its present condition is a refinement and improvement as regards vegetable, animal, and man,—is not this the suggestion, the hint, the proof, of a still greater refinement and improvement for the future; a refinement and improvement going on now? Does not refinement imply greater power, as the greater power of the crude iron comes out in steel; and are not these greater and as yet almost unrecognized powers to come out of the highest and most complex form of known organization, man; and are all of man's powers yet known?

Internally, secretly, among the thinking thousands of this and other lands, is this and many other questions now being asked: "Why must we so wither and decay, and lose the best that life is worth living for, just as we have gained that experience and wisdom that best fits us to live?" The voice of the people is always at first a whispered voice. The prayer or demand or desire of the masses is always at first a secret prayer, demand, wish, or desire, which one man at first dare scarcely whisper to his neighbour for fear of ridicule. But it is a law of Nature, that every demand, silent or spoken, brings its supply of the thing wished for in proportion to the intensity of the wish, and the growing numbers so wishing; who, by the action of their minds upon some one subject, set in motion that silent force of thought, not as yet heeded in the world's schools of philosophy, which brings the needed supply.

Millions so wished in silence for means to travel more rapidly, to send intelligence more rapidly; and this brought steam and the electric telegraph. Soon other questions and demands are to be answered, questions ever going out in silence from multitudes; and, in answering them, in at first attempting to carry out and prove the answers and the means shown to accomplish or realise many things deemed impossible or visionary, there will be mistake and stupidity, and blunder and silliness, and breakdowns and failures, and consequent ridicule; just as there were ten smashes on railways, and ten bursted boilers in the earlier era of the use of steam, to one of today. But a truth always goes straight ahead despite mistake and blunder, and proves itself at last.

There are two kinds of age,—the age of your body, and the age of your mind. Your body in a sense is but a growth, a construction, of today, and for the use of today. Your mind is another growth or construction millions of years old. It has used many bodies in its growth. It has grown from very small beginnings to its present condition, power, and capacity in the use of these many bodies. You have, in using these bodies, been far ruder and coarser than you are now. You have lived as now you could not live at all, and in forms of life or expression very different from the form you are now using; and each new body or young body you have worn has been a new suit of clothes for your mind; and what you call "death" has been and is but the wearing out of this suit through ignorance of the means, not so much of keeping it in repair, as of building it continually into a newer and newer freshness and vitality.

You are not young relatively. Your present youth means that your body is young. The older your spirit, the better can you preserve the youth, vigour, and elasticity of your body. Because the older your mind, the more power has it gathered from its many existences. You can use that power for the preservation of beauty, of health, of vigour, of all that can make you attractive to others. You can also unconsciously use the same power to make you ugly, unhealthy, weak, diseased, and unattractive. The more you use this power in either of these directions, the more will it make you ugly or beautiful, healthy or unhealthy, attractive or unattractive; that is, as regards unattractiveness for this one existence. Ultimately you must, if not in this in some other existence, be symmetrical; because the evolution of the mind, of which the evolution of our bodies from coarser to higher forms is but a crude counterpart, is ever toward the higher, finer, better, and happier.

That power is your thought. Every thought of yours is a thing as real, though you cannot see it with the physical, or outer eye, as a tree, a flower, a fruit. Your thoughts are continually moulding your muscles into shapes and manner of movement in accordance with their character.

If your thought is always determined and decided, your step in walking will be decided. If your thought is permanently decided, your whole carriage, bearing, and address will show that if you say a thing you mean it.

If your thoughts are permanently undecided, you will have a permanently undecided gesture, address, carriage, or manner of using your body; and this, when long continued, will make the body grow decidedly misshapen in some way, exactly as when you are writing in a mood of hurry, your hurried thought makes misshapen letters, and sometimes misshapen ideas; while your reposeful mood or thought makes well-formed letters and graceful curves as well as well-formed and graceful ideas.

You are every day thinking yourself into some phase of character and facial expression, good or bad. If your thoughts are permanently cheerful, your face will look cheerful. If most of the time you are in a complaining, peevish, quarrelsome mood, this kind of thought will put ugly lines on your face; they will poison your blood, make you dyspeptic, and ruin your complexion; because then you are in your own unseen laboratory of mind, generating an unseen end poisonous element, your thought; and as you put it out or think it, by the inevitable Law of nature it attracts to it the same kind of thought-elemunt from others. You think or open your mind to the mood of despondency or irritability, and you draw more or less of the same thought-element from every despondent or irritable man or woman in your town or city. You are then charging your magnet, your mind, with its electric thought-current of destructive tendency, and the law and property of thought connects all the other thought-currents of despondency or irritability with your mental battery, your mind. If we think murder or theft, we bring ourselves by this law into spiritual relationship and rapport with every thief or murderer in the world.

Your mind can make your body sick or well, strong or weak, according to the thought it puts out, and the action upon it of the thought of others. Cry "Fire!" in a crowded theatre, and scores of persons are made tremulous, weak, paralyzed by fear. Perhaps it was a false alarm. It was only the thought of fire, a horror acting on your body, that took away its strength.

The thought or mood of fear has in cases so acted on the body as to turn the hair white in a few hours.

Angered, peevish, worried, or irritable thought effects injuriously the digestion. A sudden mental shock may lose one's whole appetite for a meal, or cause the stomach to reject such meal when eaten. The injury so done the body suddenly, in a relatively few cases, by fear or other evil state of mind, works injury more gradually on millions of bodies all over the planet.

Dyspepsia does not come so much of the food we eat, as of the thoughts we think while eating it. We may eat the healthiest bread in the world; and if we eat it in a sour temper, we will put sourness in our blood, and sourness in our stomachs, and sourness on our faces. Or if we eat in an anxious frame of mind, and are worrying all the time about how much we should eat or should not eat, and whether it may not hurt us after all, we are consuming anxious, worried, fretful thought-element with our food and it will poison us. If we are cheerful and chatty and lively and jolly while eating, we are putting liveliness and cheer into ourselves, and making such qualities more and more a part of ourselves. And if our family group eat in silence, or come to the table with a sort of forced and resigned air, as if saying, each one to him or herself, "Well, all this must be gone over again;" and the head of the family buries himself in his business cares, or his newspaper, and reads all the murders and suicides and burglaries and scandals for the last twenty-four hours; and the queen of the household buries herself in sullen resignation or household cares, then there are being literally consumed at that table, along with the food, the thought-element of worry and murder and suicide and the morbid element, which loves to dwell on the horrible and ghastly; and, as a result, dyspepsia, in some of its many forms, will be manufactured all the way down the line, from one end of the table to the other.

If the habitual expression of a face be a scowl, it is because the thoughts behind that face are mostly scowls. If the corners of a mouth are turned down, it is because most of the time the thoughts which govern and shape that mouth are gloomy and despondent. If a face does not invite people, and make them desire to get acquainted with its wearer, it is because that face is a sign advertising thoughts behind it which the wearer may not dare to speak to others, possibly may not dare to whisper to himself.

The continual mood of hurry, that is, of being in mind or spirit in a certain place long before the body is there, will cause the shoulders to stoop forward; because in such mood you do literally send your thought, your spirit, your real though invisible self, to the place toward which your power, your thought, is dragging your body head first and through such life-long habit of mind does the body grow as the thought shapes it. A "self-contained" man is never in a hurry; and a self-contained man keeps or contains his thought, his spirit, his power, mostly on the act or use he is making at the present moment with the instrument his spirit uses, his body; and the habitually self-possessed woman will be graceful in every movement, for the reason that her spirit has complete possession and command of its tool, the body; and is not a mile or ten miles away from that body in thought, and fretting or hurrying or dwelling on something at that distance from her body.

When we form a plan for any business, any invention, any undertaking, we are making something of that unseen element, our thought, as real, though unseen, as any machine of iron or wood. That plan or thought begins, as soon as made, to draw to itself, in more unseen elements, power to carry itself out, power to materialize itself in physical or visible substance. When we dread a misfortune, or live in fear of any ill, or expect ill luck, we make also a construction of unseen element, thought,—which, by the same law of attraction, draws to it destructive, and to you damaging, forces or elements. Thus the law for success is also the law for misfortune, according as it is used; even as the force of a man's arm can save another from drowning, or strike a dagger to his heart. Of whatever possible thing we think, we are building, in unseen substance, a construction which will draw to us forces or elements to aid us or hurt us, according to the character of thought we think or put out.

If you expect to grow old, and keep ever in your mind an image or construction of yourself as old and decrepit, you will assuredly be so. You are then making yourself so.

If you make a plan in thought, in unseen element, for yourself, as helpless, and decrepit, such plan will draw to you of unseen thought-element that which will make you weak, helpless, and decrepit. If, on the contrary, you make for yourself a plan for being always healthy, active, and vigorous, and stick to that plan, and refuse to grow decrepit, and refuse to believe the legions ot people who will tell you that you must grow old, you will not grow old. It is because you think it must be so, as people tell you, that makes it so.

If you in your mind are ever building an ideal of yourself as strong, healthy, and vigorous, you are building to yourself of invisible element that which is ever drawing to you more of health, strength, and vigour. You can make of your mind a magnet to attract health or weakness. If you love to think of the strong things in Nature, of granite mountains and heaving billows and resistless tempests, you attract to you their elements of strength.

If you build yourself in health and strength today, and despond and give up such thinking or building tomorrow, you do not destroy what in spirit and of spirit you have built up. That amount of element so added to your spirit can never be lost but you do, for the time, in so desponding, that is, thinking weakness, stop the building of your health-structure; and although your spirit is so much the stronger for that addition of element, it may not be strong enough to give quickly to the body what you may have taken from it through such despondent thought.

Persistency in thinking health, in imagining or idealizing yourself as healthy, vigorous, and symmetrical, is the cornerstone of health and beauty. Of that which you think most, that you will be, and that you will have most of. You say "No." But your bed-ridden patient is not thinking, "I am strong;" he or she is thinking, "I am so weak." Your dyspeptic man or woman is not thinking, "I will have a strong stomach." They are ever saying, "I can't digest anything;" and they can't, for that very reason.

We are apt to nurse our maladies rather than nurse ourselves. We want our maladies petted and sympathized with, more than ourselves. When we have a bad cold, our very cough sometimes says to others, unconsciously, "I am this morning an object for your sympathy. I am so afflicted!" It is the cold, then, that is calling out for sympathy. Were the body treated rightly, your own mind and all the minds about you would say to that weak element in you, "Get out of that body!" and the silent force of a few minds so directed would drive that weakness out. It would leave as Satan did when the man of Nazareth imperiously ordered him. Colds and all other forms of disease are only forms of Satan, and thrive also by nursing. Vigour and health are catching also as well as the measles.

What would many grown-up people give for a limb or two limbs that had in them the spring and elasticity of those owned by a boy twelve years old; for two limbs that could climb trees, walk on rail fences, and run because they loved to run, and couldn't help running? If such limbs so full of life could be manufactured and sold, would there not be a demand for them by those stout ladies and gentlemen who get in and out of their carriages as if their bodies weighed a ton? Why is it that humanity resigns itself with scarcely a protest to the growing heaviness, sluggishness, and stiffness that comes even with middle age? I believe, however, we compromise with this inertia, and call it dignity. Of course a man and a father and a citizen and a voter and a pillar of the State—of inertia—shouldn't run and cut up and kick up like a boy, because he can't. Neither should a lady who has grown to the dignity of a waddle run as she did when a girl of twelve, because she can't, either. Actually we put on our infirmities as we would masks, and hobble around in them, saying, "This is the thing to do, because we can't do anything else." Sometimes we are even in a hurry to put them on; like the young gentleman who sticks an eye-glass to his eye, and thereby the sooner ruins the sight of a sound organ, in order to look tony or bookish.

There are more and more possibilities In Nature, in the elements, and in man and out of man; and they come as fast as man sees and knows how to use these forces in Nature and in himself. Possibilities and miracles mean the same thing.

The telephone sprung suddenly on "our folks" of two hundred years ago would have been a miracle, and might have consigned the person using it to the prison or the stake: all unusual manifestations of Nature's powers being then attributed to the Devil, because the people of that period had so much of the Devil, or cruder element, in them as to insist that the universe should not continually show and prove higher and higher expressions of the higher mind for man's comfort and pleasure.

Museum and Menagerie Horrors

A Menagerie of beasts and birds means a collection of captured walking and flying creatures, taken from their natural modes of life, deprived permanently of such modes, and suffering more or less in consequence. The bird, used to the freedom of forest and air is imprisoned in the most limited quarters. Its plumage there is never as fresh and glossy as in its natural state. It does not live as long. The captive life of the many species brought from the tropics is very short, especially of the smaller and more delicate species.

Bears, lions, tigers, deer, wolves and all other animals like liberty and freedom of range as well as man. In the menagerie they are deprived of it. The air they breathe is often fetid and impure. To the burrowing animal, earth is as much a necessity and comfort as a comfortable bed is to us. The captured burrower is often kept on a hard board floor, which, in its restless misery to get into its native earth, it scratches and wears away in cavities inches in depth.

Monkeys by the thousand die prematurely of consumption, because forced to live in a climate too cold and damp for them, and no amount of artificial heat can supply the element to which they have been accustomed in the air of their native tropic groves and jungles.

Seals are kept in tanks of fresh water, when salt water is their natural element. Their captive lives are always short.

There is no form of organized life but is a part and belonging of the locality and latitude where in its wild state it is born. The polar bear is a natural belonging of the Arctic regions. The monkey is a belonging and outgrowth of tropical conditions. When either of these is taken from climes native to them, and out of which they do not voluntarily wander, pain is inflicted on them.

Go to the cheap "museum," now so plentiful, and regard the bedraggled plumage and apparent sickly condition of many of the birds, natives of distant climes, imprisoned there. You see them but for an hour. Return in a few months and you will not find them. What has become of them. They have died, and their places are supplied by others likewise slowly dying. The procession of captives so to suffer and die prematurely never ceases moving into these places. Ships are constantly bringing them hither. An army of men distributed all over the world, and ranging through the forests of every clime, is constantly engaged in trapping them. For what reasons are all these concentrations of captured misery, now to be found in every large town and city of our country? 7 Simply to gratify human curiosity. Simply that we may stand a few minutes and gaze at them behind their bars. What do we then learn of their real natures and habits in these prisons? What would be learned of your real tastes, inclinations and habits were you kept constantly in a cage?

Is the gratification of this curiosity worth the misery it costs?

If a bird wooed by your kindness comes and builds its nest in a tree near your window, and there rears its brood, is not the sight it affords from day to day worth a hundred times more than that of the same bird, deprived of its mate and shut up in a cage? Will you not, is in its freedom you study its real habits and see its real and natural life, feel more and more drawn to it by the tie of a common sympathy, as you see evidenced in that life so much that belongs to your own? Like you, it builds a home; like you, it has affection and care for its mate; like you, it provides for its family; like you, it is alarmed at the approach of danger; like you, it nestles in the thought of security.

Yet so crude and cruel still is the instinct in our race, that the ruin of the wild bird's home, or its slaughter or capture, is the ruling desire with nineteen boys out of twenty as they roam the woods; and "cultured parents" will see their children leave the house equipped with the means for this destruction without even the thought of protest.

The God in Yourself

As a spirit, you are a part of God or the Infinite Force or Spirit of good. As such part, you are an ever-growing power which can never lessen, and must always increase, even as it has in the past through many ages always increased, and built you up, as to intelligence, to your present mental stature. The power of your mind has been growing to its present quality and clearness through many more physical lives than the one you are now living. Through each past life you have unconsciously added to its power. Every struggle of the mind—be it struggle against pain, struggle against appetite, struggle for more skill in the doing of anything, struggle for greater advance in any art or calling, struggle and dissatisfaction at your failings and defects—is an actual pushing of the spirit to greater power, and a greater relative completion of yourself,—and with such completion, happiness. For the aim of living is happiness.

There is today more of you, and more of every desirable mental quality belonging to you, than ever before. The very dissatisfaction and discontent you may feel concerning your failings is a proof of this. If your mind was not as clear as it is, it could not see those failings. You are not now where you may have been in a mood of self-complacency, when you thought yourself about right in every respect. Only you may, now, in looking at yourself, have swung too far in the opposite direction; and, because your eyes have been suddenly opened to certain faults, you may think these faults to be constantly increasing. They are not. The God in yourself—the ever-growing power in yourself—has made you see an incompleteness in your character; yet that incompleteness was never so near a relative completion as now. Of this the greatest proof is, that you can now see what in yourself you never saw or felt before.

You may have under your house a cavity full of vermin and bad air. You were much worse off before the cavity was found, repulsive as it may be to you; and now that it is found, you may be sure it will be cleansed. There may be cavities in our mental architecture abounding in evil element, and there is no need to be discouraged as the God in our self shows them to us. There is no need of saying, " I'm such an imperfect creature I'm sure I can never cure all my faults." Yes, you can. You are curing them now. Every protest of your mind against your fault is a push of the spirit forward. Only you must not expect to cure them all in an hour, a day, a week, or a year. There will never be a time in your future existence, but that you can see where you can improve yourself. If you see possibility of improvement, you must of course see the defect to be improved. Or, in other words, you see for yourself a still greater completion, a still greater elaboration, a finer and finer shading of your character, a more and more complicated distribution of the Force always coming to you. So you will cease this fretting over your being such an imperfect creature when you find, as you will, that you are one of the " temples of God " ever being built by yourself into ever-increasing splendour.

No talent of yours ever stops growing any more than the tree stops growing in winter. If you are learning to paint or draw or act or speak in public or do anything, and cease your practice entirely for a month or a year or two years, and then take it up again, you will find after a little that an increase of that talent has come; that you have new ideas concerning it, and new power for execution.

You ask, "What is the aim of life?" In a sense, you cannot aim your own life. There is a destiny that aims it,—a law which governs and carries it. To what? To an ever-increasing and illimitable capacity for happiness as your power increases, and increase it must. You cannot stop growing, despite all appearances to the contrary. The pain you have suffered has been through that same growth of the spirit pressing you harder and harder against what caused you misery, so that at last you should take that pain as a proof that you were on some wrong path, out of which you must get as soon as possible; and when you cry out hard, and are in living earnest to know the right way, something will always come to tell you the right way; for it is a law of nature that every earnest call is answered, and an earnest demand or prayer for anything always brings the needed supply.

What is the aim of life? To get the most happiness out of it; to so learn to live that every coming day will be looked for in the assurance that it will be as full, and even fuller, of pleasure than the day we now live in; to banish even the recollection that time can hang heavily on our hands; to be thankful that we live; to rise superior to sickness or pain; to command the body, through the power of the spirit, so that it can feel no pain; to control and command the thought so that It shall ever increase in power to work and act separate, apart, and afar from our body, so that it shall bring us all that we need of house or land or food or clothes, and that without robbing or doing injustice to anyone; to gain in power so that the spirit shall ever recuperate, reinvigorate, and rejuvenate the body so long as we desire to use it, so that no part or organ shall weaken, wither, or decay; to be learning ever new sources of amusement for ourselves and others; to make ourselves so full of happiness and use for others, that our presence may ever be welcome to them; to be no one's enemy and every one's friend,—that is the destiny of life in those domains of existence where people as real as we, and much more alive than we, have learned, and are ever learning, how to get the most of heaven out of life. That is the inevitable destiny of every individual spirit.

You cannot escape ultimate happiness and permanent happiness as you grow on and on in this and other existences; and all the pains you suffer, or have suffered, are as prods and pokes to keep you out of wrong paths,—to make you follow the law. And the more sensitive you grow, the more clearly will you see the law which leads away from all pain, and ever toward more happiness, and to a state of mind where it is such an ecstasy to live, that all sense of time is lost,—as the sense of time is lost with us when we are deeply interested or amused, or gaze upon a thrilling play or spectacle,—so that in the words of the biblical record, "a day shall be as a thousand years, and a thousand years as a day."

The Nirvana of the Hindus suggests all the possibilities of life coming to our planet,—"Nirvana " implying that calmness, serenity, and confidence of mind which comes of the absolute certainty that every effort we make, every enterprise we undertake, must be successful; and that the happiness we realize this month is but the stepping-stone to the greater happiness of next. If you fell that the trip of foreign travel you now long for and wish for was as certain to come as now you are certain that the sun rose this morning; if you knew that you would achieve your own peculiar and individual proficiency and triumph in painting or oratory, or as an actor or sculptor, or in any art, as surely as now you know you can walk downstairs, you would not of course feel any uneasiness. In all our relatively perfected lives we shall know this, because we shall know for an absolute certainty that when we concentrate our mental force or thought on any plan or pursuit or undertaking, we are setting at work the attractive force of thought- substance to draw to us the means or agencies or forces or individuals to carry out that plan, as certainly as the force of muscle applied to a line draws the ship to its pier.

You worry very little now as to your telegram reaching its destination, because, while you know next to nothing as to what electricity is, you do know that when it is applied in a certain way it will carry your message; and you will have the same confidence that when your thought is regulated and directed by a certain method, it will do for you what you wish. Before men knew how to use electricity there was as much of it as today, and with the same power as today; but so far as our convenience was concerned, it was quite useless as a message-bearer. lack of knowledge to direct it. The tremendous power of human thought is with us all today very much in a similar condition. It is wasted, because we do not know how to concentrate and direct it. It is worse than wasted, because, through ignorance and life-long habit, we work our mental batteries in the wrong direction, and send from us bolt after bolt of ill-will toward others, or enviousness or snarls or sneers or some form of ugliness,—all this being real element wrongly and ignorantly applied, which may strike and hurt others, and will certainly hurt us.

Here is the cornerstone of all successful effort in this existence or any other. Never in thought acknowledge an impossibility. Never in mind reject what to you may seem the wildest idea with scorn; because, in so doing, you may not know what you are closing the door against. To say anything is impossible because it seems impossible to you, is just so much training in the dangerous habit of calling out "Impossible!" to every new idea. Your mind is then a prison full of doors, barred to all outside, and you the only inmate. "All things" are possible with God. God works in and through you. To say " Impossible!" as to what you may do or become is a sin. It is denying God's power to work through you. It is denying the power of the Infinite Spirit to do through you far more than what you are now capable of conceiving in mind. To say "Impossible!" is to set up your relatively weak limit of comprehension as the standard of the universe. It is as audacious as to attempt the measurement of endless space with a yard-stick.

When you say "Impossible!" and "I can't" you make a present impossibility for yourself. This thought of yours is the greatest hindrance to the possible. It cannot stop it. You will be pushed on, hang back as much as you may. There can be no successful resistance to the eternal and constant betterment of all things (including yourself).

You should say, "It is possible for me to become anything which I admire." You should say, " It is possible for me to become a writer, an orator, an actor, an artist." You have then thrown open the door to your own temple of art within you. So long as you said "Impossible!" you kept it closed. Your "I can't" was the iron bolt locking that door against you. Your "I can" is the power shoving back that bolt.

Christ's spirit or thought had power to command the elements, and quiet the storm. Your spirit as a part of the great whole has in the germ, and waiting for fruition, the same power. Christ, through power of concentrating the unseen element of his thought, could turn that unseen element into the seen, and materialize food,—loaves and fishes. That is a power inherent in every spirit, and every spirit is growing to such power. You see today a healthy baby-boy. It cannot lift a pound; but you know there lies in that feeble child the powers and possibilities which, twenty years hence, may enable it to lift with ease two hundred pounds. So the greater power, the coming spiritual power, can be foretold for us, who are now relatively babes spiritually. The reason for life's being so unhappy here in this region of being is, that as we do not know the law, we go against it, and get thereby its pains instead of its pleasures.

The law cannot be entirely learned by us out of past record or the past experience of anyone, no matter to what power they might have attained. Such records or lives may be very useful to us as suggesters. But while there are general principles that apply to all, there are also individual laws that apply to every separate and individualized person. You cannot follow directly in my track in making yourself happier and better, nor can I in yours; because every one of us is made up of a different combination of element, as element has entered into and formed our spirits (our real selves) through the growth and evolution ages. You must study and find out for yourself what your nature requires to bring it permanent happiness. You are a book for yourself. You must open this book page after page, and chapter after chapter, as they come to you with the experience of each day, each month, each year, and read them. No one else can read them for you as you can for yourself. No one else can think exactly as you think, or feel just as you feel, or be affected just as you are affected by otter forces or persons about you; and for this reason no other person can judge what you really need to make your life more complete, more perfect, more happy so well as yourself.

You must find out for yourself what association is best for you, what food is best for you, and what method in any business, any art, any profession brings you the best results. You can be helped very much by conferring with others who are similarly interested. You can be very much helped by those who may have more knowledge than you of general laws. You can be greatly helped to get force or courage or new ideas to carry out your undertakings, by meeting at regular intervals with earnest, sincere, and honest people who have also some definite purpose to accomplish, and talking yourself out to them, and they to you. But when you accept any man or any woman as an infallible guide or authority, and do exactly as they say, you are off the main track; because then you are making the experiments of another person, formed of a certain combination of elements or chemicals, and the result of that person's experiments, the rule for your own individual combination of element, when your combination may be very different, and differently acted on by the elements outside of it.

You have iron and copper and magnesia and phosphorus, and more of other minerals and chemicals, and combination and re-combination of mineral and chemical, in your physical body than earthly science has yet thought of. You have in your spirit or thought the unseen or spiritual correspondences of these minerals still finer and more subtle; and all these are differently combined, and in different proportions, from any other physical or spiritual body. How, then, can anyone find out the peculiar action of this your individual combination, save yourself?

There are certain general laws; but every individual must apply the general law to him or herself. It is a general law that the wind will propel a ship. But every vessel does not use the air in exactly the same fashion. It is a general law that thought is force, and can effect, and is constantly effecting, results to others far from our bodies; and the quality of our thought and its power to affect results depends very much on our associations. But for that reason, if yours is the superior thought or power, and I see that through its use you are moving ahead in the world, I should not choose your character of associates or your manner of life. I can try your methods as experiments; but I must remember they are only experiments. I must avoid that so common error,—the error of slavish copy and idolatry of another.

The Christ of Nazareth once bade certain of his followers not to worship him. "Call me not good," said he. "There is none good save God alone." Christ said, "I am the way and the life," meaning, as the text interprets itself to me, that as to certain general laws of which he was aware, and by which he also as a spirit was governed, he knew and could give certain information. But he never did assert that his individual life, with all the human infirmity or defect that he had "taken upon him," was to be strictly copied. He did pray to the Infinite Spirit of Good for more strength, and deliverance from the SIN OF FEAR when his spirit quailed at the prospect of his crucifixion; and in so doing, he conceded that he, as a spirit (powerful as he was), needed help as much as any other spirit; and knowing this, he refused to pose himself before his followers as God, or the Infinite, but told them that when they desired to bow before that almighty and never-to-be-comprehended power, out of which comes every good at the prayer or demand of human mind, to worship God alone,—God, the eternal and unfathomable moving power of boundless universe; the power that no man has ever seen or ever will see, save as he sees its varying expressions in sun, star, cloud, wind, bird, beast, flower, animal, or in man as the future angel or archangel, and ascending still to grades of mind and grades of power higher and higher still; but ever and ever looking to the source whence comes their power, and never, never worshipping any one form of such expression, and by so doing making the " creature greater than the Creator."

That power is today working on and in and through every man, woman, and child on this planet. Or, to use the biblical expression, it is, "God working in us and through us." We are all parts of the Infinite Power,—a power ever carrying us up to higher, finer, happier grades of being.

Every man or woman, no matter what may be their manner of life or grade of intellect, is a stronger and better man or woman than ever they were before, despite all seeming contradiction. The desire in human nature, and all forms of nature or of spirit expressed through matter, to be more and more refined is, up to a certain growth of mind, an unconscious desire. The god desire is at work on the lowest drunkard rolling in the gutter. That man's spirit wants to get out of the gutter. Ii is at work on the greatest liar, prompting him, if ever so feebly, that the truth is better. It is at work on people you may call despicable and vile. When Christ was asked how often a man should be forgiven any offence, he replied in a manner indicating that there should be no limit to the sum of one man or woman's forgiveness for the defects or immaturity in another. There should be no limit to the kind and helpful thought we think or put out toward another person who falls often, who is struggling with some unnatural appetite. It is a great evil, often done unconsciously, to say or think of an intemperate man, " Oh, he's gone to the dogs. It's no use doing anything more for him!" because, when we do this, we put hopeless, discouraging thought out in the air. It meets that person. He or she will feel it; and it is to them an element retarding their progress out of the slough they are in, just as some person's similar thought has retarded us in our effort to get out of some slough we were in or are in now,—slough of indecision; slough of despondency; slough of ill-temper; slough of envious, hating thought.

Yet the spirit of man becomes the stronger for all it struggles against. It becomes the stronger for struggling against your censorious, uncharitable thought, until at last it carries a man or woman to a point where they may in thought say to others, "I would rather have your approbation than your censure. But I am not dependent on your approbation or censure, for my most rigid judge and surest punishment for all the evil I do comes of my own mind,—the god or goddess in myself from whose judgment, from whose displeasure, there is no escaping." Yet as the spirit grows clearer and clearer in sight, so does that judge in ourselves become more and more merciful for its own errors; for it knows that, in a sense, as we refine from cruder to finer expression, there must be just so much evil to be contended against, fought against, and finally and inevitably overcome. Every man and woman is predestined to a certain amount of defect, until the spirit overcomes such defect; and overcome it must, for it is the nature of spirit to struggle against defect. It is the one thing impossible for man to take this quality out of his own spirit—the quality of ever rising toward more power and happiness.

If you make this an excuse to sin, or commit excess, or lie or steal or murder, and say, "I can't help it; I'm predestined to it," you will be punished all the same, not possibly by man's law, but by natural or divine law which has its own punishments for every possible sin,—for murder or lust or lying or stealing or evil thinking or gluttony; and these punishments are being constantly inflicted, and today thousands on thousands are suffering for the sins they commit in ignorance of the law of life; and the pain of such punishment has grown so great, and bears so heavily on so many, that there is now a greater desire than ever to know more of these laws; and for that very reason is this desire being met, and these questions are being answered; for it is an inevitable law of nature that what the human mind demands, that it, in time, gets; and the greater the number of minds so demanding, the sooner is the demand met, and the questions answered. Steam but a few years ago relatively met the demand of human mind for greater speed in travel. Electricity met a demand for greater speed in sending intelligence from man to man. These are but as straws pointing to the discovery and use of greater powers, not only in elements outside of man, but in the unseen elements which make man and woman; in the elements unseen which make you and me.

Henceforth our race will commence to be lifted out of evil or cruder forms of expression, not by fear ot the punishments coming through violation of the law, but they will be led to the wiser course through love of the delight which comes of following the law as we discover it for ourselves. You eat moderately, because experience has taught that the greater pleasure comes of moderation. You are gentle, kind, and considerate to your friend, not that you have constantly before your mind the fear of losing that friend if you are not kind and considerate, but because it pleases you, and you love the doing of kind acts. Human law, and even divine law as interpreted by human understanding, have ever been saying in the past, "You must not do this or that, or you'll feel the rod." God has been pictured as a stern, merciless, avenging deity. The burden of the preacher's song has been Penalty and Punishment! Punishment and Penalty! Humanity is to forget all about penalty and punishment, because it is to be won over, and tempted to greater goodness, to purity and refinement by the ever-increasing pleasures brought us as we refine. The warning of penalty was necessary when humanity was cruder. It could only be reached by the rod. The race was blind, and as a necessity of its condition it had to be kept somewhere near the right path by a succession of painful prods and pokes with the sharp goad of penalty. But when we begin to see clearer, as now the more quickened and sensitive of our race do begin to see, we need no rod, anymore than you need a man with a club to prevail on you to go to a feast.

The Healing and Renewing Force of Spring

Your body is acted on in its growth and changes by the same laws and elements which govern the growth and enter into all other organized bodies, such as trees, plants, birds, and animals.

In the early spring of every year, there comes and acts on this planet a force from the sun which affects all organized forms of life,—trees, birds, animals, and, above all, man. Man's being the highest, most complicated, and most powerful mental organism on the planet, absorbs the most of this power, and will absorb far more in the future, and to far greater advantage than at present, as he learns to place himself in the best states to receive it.

Material science calls this force "heat"; but the quality known as heat is only its outward or physical manifestation. The quality known as heat which comes from the sun is not converted into heat until it reaches our planet and acts on the earth elements. There is little or no heat a few miles above the earth's surface. Were this force in the form of heat on leaving the sun, or during its passage, the air on the mountain tops would be as warm as that of the valleys. As we know, on the highest peaks snow and ice are perpetual, for the sun-force at such elevation is not sufficiently mingled with earth elements to convert it into that degree of heat felt in the valleys and plains.

This force causes the the increased movement and circulation of sap in the trees, which commences as soon as the sun of the new year acts on them. The sap is a new life to the tree, from which later comes its buds, blossoms, and fruitage. The inflowing of this unseen sun-force gives the tree power to draw new supplies of nourishing elements through its roots from the earth. It gives it power also to cast off any dead leaves remaining of the last year's crop which have hung on during the winter, as you may see in forests of oak or hickory.

This force acts also in the later winter and earlier spring months on animals and birds, especially if in their wild or natural state, causing them to shed their last year's coats of fur or feathers. But this casting off of old visible matter is but a relatively small part of the change going on within them. There is also a casting out or shedding of old invisible matter throughout the bird or animal's entire body. It goes off through the pores or other passages in various forms, some visible, others invisible, and is succeeded by new elements within, as the new fur, hair or feather is grown without.

Your body is governed by the same law. During the later winter and earlier spring months, you are "moulting." You are casting off old, dead matter, and taking in new, providing you give this force opportunity to act on you to the best advantage, by ceasing to be active either with mind or body when they call for rest, as do birds and animals during their moulting period, or process of casting off the old elements and receiving the new.

This element or force received at this time by you and them is invisible to the physical eye, as all force is invisible. The new fur, the new plumage of the bird, the new skin and tissues without and within your body, if received, the new buds, leaves, and twigs, are all materialized expressions of this force. They are new crystalizations coming of a new solution of invisible chemicals, in which bird, animal, tree, and your body are bathed. All of last year's solution or elements so absorbed have been used up. The tree or other visible organization of bird, animal, or your body, stands in the same relation to this re-clothing solution as does the slip of metal in the solution of mineral which attracts out of such solution the crystallizations which form on it.

There is no great dividing line betwixt what we call matter and spirit. Matter is but a form of spirit or thought seen of the physical eye. Matter is force temporarily materialized, as in the lump of coal which, when set on fire, sends off the force bound up in it to move the engine. The lump passes then mostly into element invisible. So all about us we find force ever passing from physical visibility into invisibility, and vice versa. Millions on millions of tons of invisible matter may be on a clear day suspended over our heads one hour, the next to fall in the visible form of rain or snow, which a few hours after may be drawn upward again, but invisible.

The Indian called February and March the "weak months," recognizing, as he did, being a closer observer of nature than we, the tendency to sluggishness and inactivity in animal and man, which always prevails when this power is recuperating, and renewing any organized body.

The most perfect crystallizations out of mineral element come of the solution kept most free from agitation. Your body is governed by the same law in this spring renewing and re-crystallization of its elements. To receive the fullest benefit of the heating and renewing element of spring, you should rest whenever you feel like resting, whether it be the middle of the day or the middle of the night. If you keep the body or mind at work against their inclination—if you force your muscles to exertion through mere strength of will—if you work with either mind or body to the verge of utter exhaustion, not knowing how depleted you are of strength until your work is over, as thousands on thousands do and are compelled to do, through our unnatural system of life and the arbitrary demands of "business," you prevent this healing and recuperative power from acting to its fullest extent on the body. You prevent the new element, which is renewing the tree and causing the buds to swell, from assimilating with your body. You hold on to worn-out element which should be cast off as the oak has cast all its dead leaves before the winter is over; you carry, then, this dead element, a "dead weight," about with you, instead of the new and upward rising life. It is this, among other causes, which stoops the shoulders, bleaches the hair, and furrows the face with wrinkles, through shrinkage of tissues.

The decay of the physical body which we call "old age," is owing entirely to man's neither believing nor knowing that he can place himself in the proper conditions to receive a never-ceasing supply of force, which would reclothe the spirit constantly with new material. Mere muscular strength and constant activity of body are not always signs of the most perfect health. In the delirium of fever a relatively weak man may require two or three others to hold him. When this delirium has passed away, he is weak as an infant, yet often, the crisis being passed, is pronounced out of danger. In a manner somewhat similar in the walks of business, in the keen, almost fierce competition of trade, thousands of people lead a feverish, excited life. They are always on a tension. They demand to be in this state. They cannot work unless "strung up" to a certain pitch. If, at times, through nature's own demand for rest, their nerves are relaxed and they feel languid, they mistake this friendly signal for some form of disease, and treat it accordingly.

Even in these cases, when laid for weeks or months on sick-beds, and nursed through what is called a "dangerous illness," and believing it to be one, they sometimes come out at last better and stronger than they had been for a long period previous. Why? Because through this enforced cessation from physical or mental activity, nature was working as well as she could under certain unfavourable circumstances, rebuilding a worn-out body, and as a result the man arose with new, fresh element in his bones, muscles, and nerves, put there because nature had then his body laid up in quiet, so that it could be repaired.

If you will but entertain this idea of spring's renewing force respectfully, though you cannot believe it thoroughly at first, you will receive much help by such respectful entertainment; for if you do not kick a live truth out of your mind when it first presents itself, it will take root and live there, and prove itself by doing you good.

Men, through incessant physical toil, wear out far sooner than is generally realized. The hardy sailor's "hardiness" often lasts but a few years. He is often an old man at forty-five. The toiling farmer, who works the year round from early dawn till dark, and thinks work to be the greatest virtue in the world, is often a mass of bony knobs and rheumatism at fifty. The average duration of lives of hard labour is much less than those given to occupations requiring less physical lugging, straining, and fagging, hour after hour, when the body is really exhausted.

In the mines of California, where I swung a pick for years, and worked with gangs of men, lifting, wheeling, and shovelling, I noted that the last three hours of a day's work of ten and sometimes twelve hours' length, was done by the men, strong as they might be, with far less spirit than the earlier day's labour,—in fact it was often a mere pretence of work, unless the watchful eye of the "boss" was constantly on his men. Why? Because physically they were no longer fit to work. It was only will that was urging muscle to exertion. And of the stout, "hardy" miners, aged twenty- five or thereabout, who were so working in 1860, and who persisted in such drudgery, a large majority are dead, and of those who are alive today, four-fifths are broken-down men.

In the kingdom of nature, we find periods of rest constantly alternating with periods of activity. Trees rest during the winter. The circulation of sap is sluggish. There is no creation of leaf, blossom or fruit. Wild birds and animals after the summer breeding season, do little save eat and sleep. Some animals and reptiles sleep during the entire winter. Even soil must rest to bring the best crop. Where it is forced, through constant artificial fertilization, the product is inferior in flavour and nourishing quality to that raised on "virgin soil." Disease, blight, and destructive insects some unknown to vegetation in its natural state. When man recognizes the fact that he cannot use his body year after year, from the budding strength of youth to the age of forty or fifty under such a full, unceasing pressure of nerve or will power without great injury, and when he does recognize the fact that through placing himself oftener in restful and receptive states, as do tree, bird, and animal in their natural state, he will then, through receiving far more of this element, enjoy a far greater health of body, elasticity of muscle, vigour and brilliancy of mind. He would also have other senses and powers awakened within him, whose existence is still doubted by most people.

Some Oriental and Indian races have, to an extent, the uses of these senses and powers, partly by reason of their more restful lives and their living like tree and animal, more in conformity to the influence on them of the seasons. They have not our domineering, aggressive force, which invades and conquers for a time, as England has conquered India, and our own people have subdued and almost exterminated the Indian. But mark: this force does not conquer in the end. The thought-power which works most while the body is relatively inactive, is really the strongest and ultimately prevails. It is subtle, noiseless, unseen. Working with the highest motive, it refines and polishes the rude, warlike, conquering races, by grafting on them the civilization of the conquered. In such manner was the art and civilization of conquered Egypt transferred to the Assyrian. Centuries afterward the conquered Assyrian transferred this power to conquering Greece. Greece fell before Rome, yet Grecian civilization held sway in Rome. Rome fell physically before the Goths and Vandals, the then savage races of Northern Europe; but in the kingdom of mind it is the influence of ancient Italy which has been the great factor in refining the Goth, Hun, and Vandal of ages ago into the modem

German, Frenchman, Spaniard and Italian. Every convulsion, agitation, and conquest has made this power take root on a wider field.

Today the best English mind is seriously studying the laws which at last it has recognized in India, and that force is in a sense to subdue England, for she is already sitting at the feet of India, receiving her first lessons in the alphabet of laws and force, hitherto quite unrecognized by her learned men.

"What power is this?" you ask—"How gained? How developed?" It is the power coming of minds united on one purpose, in perfect concord, and who do not use it all in physical activity. For if you put all your thought or force in the working of the members of your body, in working with your hands at any calling day in and day out, year in and year out, with no regard to the impulses and instincts of times or seasons, you keep all that force working merely the Instrument—the body—and wearing it out. You prevent it from operating at a distance from the body. You prevent also the inflowing and assimilation of this recuperative power of spring. You breed the habit of keeping the body always in motion. You prevent yourself from getting that order of sleep which would bring your body the most strength for the waking hours. For if the body or mind is fagged out day after day, the same order of thought prevails and is fagging it out by night. You breed the belief and error that you are accomplishing nothing unless at work with body or brain. You cannot get into that state of repose when your thought-power could work at a distance and apart from your body, and bring you in time a hundred-fold more of beneficial result than can ever be realized through mere physical exertion.

The quality in the plant's leaf, root, or berry, which, when taken as medicine, acts on the internal organs, is the force in that plant, liberated through the digestive process. The strength you get from bread or meat is force liberated from the food in the same manner. Digestion is a slow burning up of the material taken in the body, as coal is burned in the boiler, and the force freed by such burning you use to work the body as the engineer uses heat to run the engine. The newer the bud, the more tender is its outward material formation, yet that bud, when used medicinally, contains the most active force, principle, and quality of the plant. The choicest and strongest tea is made of the topmost and tenderest buds of the plant. In California, the bud of the poison oak affects some people though they only stand near it, so great is an injurious force it sends out in the air. The tender buds of spring contain that force which, later on, will make the more solid leaf or branch. In your own organization in the spring are the same tender, budding elements. So, if your body is weak in the spring, it is a sign that the new buds, so to speak, within you are forming. They are full of force. But that force has not had time to act on your material organization and form the new bone, muscle, and sinew which will come at a later period. providing such budding or new crystallization be not agitated, disturbed, and possibly destroyed by undue exertion of mind or body, where the same relative damage is done your body as would be done the budding tree by a hurricane.

Possibly you say, "But how can I carry on my business and earn my bread if I so lay my body up for nature's repairs?" We answer, "'The laws of man's business are not the laws of nature. If nature says 'Rest' and man says 'Work,' and will work or must work, man always gets the worst of it." What society calls vicious practices or habits are nor the only agencies which bring disease, pain, and death. Thousands perish annually in lingering agony on respectable beds, and in the "best society." Consumption, cancer, insanity, dropsy, rheumatism, scrofula, fevers, rage are ever raging among the most correct people, from the conventional standpoint. Why is this?

If you are in conditions of life where at present it is impossible to give yourself needed rest and you feel thoroughly the need of such rest, you may rely upon it that your persistent desire, your prayer, your imperious demand that you shall have opportunity to receive and profit by nature's restoring forces, will bring you in some way the opportunity to so profit by them. When any need is thoroughly felt, the thought and desire coming of such feeling is itself a prayer—a force which will bring you helps and take you out of injurious surroundings and modes of life. We repeat this assertion often. It needs frequent repetition. It is the main-spring of all growth and advance into a happier and more healthful life. The Christ of Judea embodied this great law in the words, "Ask, and ye shall receive: seek, and ye shall find, knock, and it shall be opened unto you." He wisely made no attempt to explain this mystery whereby earnest human thought, desire, or aspiration always in time brings the thing or result desired. For this and other mysteries are inexplicable, and so fast as any alleged cause is given for any certain result in nature's workings, do we find a deeper mystery in the very cause.

We say, "wind is air in motion." What sets it in motion, and keeps it in motion? Once we "explained" the tides on the theory of the moon's attraction. But apart from the tides, what power keeps in motion the gigantic system of currents ever traversing the oceans, revealed more fully during the last forty years? What power keeps our lungs breathing day and night, or the blood running to every part of the body? Are not all of these of the power of God, or the infinite spirit or force of good, working within you as it works in everything that lives and grows? Only to us is at last given the knowledge to work this power intelligently. The body of the tree, animal, and bird decays at last, through lack of such intelligence. So, in the past, has man's material part decayed. But this is not always to be. "The last great enemy to be destroyed," says Paul, "is death"; implying that as man's knowledge and faith in the wonderful forces about him and in him increased, he would discover better and better how to place himself in the line of the working of these forces, and in so doing make the mortal part immortal, through incessant renewal of finer and finer elements.

Immortality in the Flesh

We believe that immortality in the flesh is a possibility, or, in other words, that a physical body can be retained so long as the spirit desires its use, and that this body instead of decreasing in strength and vigour as the years go on will increase, and its youth will be perpetual.

We believe that the reputed fables in the ancient mythologies referring to the "immortals" or beings possessed of powers other and greater than "mortals " have a foundation in fact.

This possibility must come in accordance with the law that every demand or prayer of humanity must bring supply. There is now a more earnest demand than ever for longer and more perfect physical life, because now more minds see the greater possibilities of life. They appreciate more than ever the value of living in the physical. Such demand often takes this form of expression, " I have just learned how to live and it is nearly time for me to die."

The body will grow to these results through a gradual series of spiritual processes, operating on and ever-changing, spiritualizing and refining the material. These processes do not retain the body a person may have now. They retain "a body," and an ever changing and refining body.

All disease (lack of physical ease) or sickness comes of a spiritual process, the aim of which is reconstruction of the physical body, first in the receiving of new elements, and second in the casting out of old ones.

Back of this physical reconstruction, however, there is going on the far more important reconstruction of the spirit out of which is built the body. These processes are continually going on with the body, operating through the skin, the stomach, and other organs, as well as in the periods of physical prostration or indisposition above referred to.

All sickness is an effort of the spirit renewed by fresh influx of force to cast off old and relatively dead matter. But as this intent has not been recognized by the race, the spiritual process or effort with its accompanying pain and discomfort has been held and feared as a signal or approach of death. So with no knowledge of spiritual law, and judging everything by the material, the temporary and necessary weakness of body accompanying the process has been considered an unmitigated ill. Such belief has in the past only aided the spirit to pile on itself more and more of belief in the untruth that after a certain term of years no power or force in the universe could prevent the physical body from "ageing," shrivelling, weakening, and finally perishing.

The body is continually changing its elements in accordance with the condition of the mind. In certain mental conditions, it is adding to itself elements of decay, weakness and physical death; in another mental condition, it is adding to itself elements of strength, life and perpetual life.

That which the spirit takes on in either case are thoughts or beliefs. Thoughts and beliefs materialize themselves in flesh and blood. Belief in inevitable decay and death brings from the spirit to the body the elements of decay and death. Belief in the possibility of an ever-coming inflowing to the spirit of life brings life.

If new life is being thus added to you, there must also be an accompanying throwing off of the old or relatively dead matter of the body, just as when an influx of new life comes to the tree in the spring it casts off the dead leaves which may have clung to it all winter.

Through similar inflowing of new life or force does the animal and bird yearly shed the old fur or feathers and take on the new, and correspondent changes take place throughout the whole organization of bird, animal and man.

This spiritual law works in all forms and organizations of the cruder form of spirit we call "matter." In the human being this influx of force is greater than in the lower forms of life. It does not flow equally to all human beings. Some receive more than others. But in the course of advancement men and women are to come who will receive so much of this influx as to be obliged to see these further possibilities of existence, and also to realize them.

When new ideas or thoughts are received by our higher mind or self, they are warred against by our lower or material mind. The body is the battle ground between these two forces, and therefore suffers. As minds come to trust even to a small extent in the Supreme Power and entertain the idea that physical disease and physical death are not absolute necessities, the higher Power must prevail. Some old error will be cast out; some new idea will come to stay; the body will be better and stronger after each succeeding struggle, and these struggles will also gradually become less and less severe, until they cease altogether.

People have in the past lost their physical bodies, because, being in ignorance of the fact that sickness is a process for the spirit to throw off the old material thought and take on new, they have used their forces in the wrong way to retain such thought. They retain it by their belief. Your belief will make your sickness a benefit or an evil to you. If you can but entertain the belief that it is a spiritual process for getting rid of old worn-out elements, you assist greatly the mind in the performance of this process. If, however, you believe that sickness is entirely a physical condition, and that no benefit and only evil comes of it, you are using force only to load down the spirit with more and more error of which your flesh and blood will be in quality an expression, until at last your spirit rejects the body it has been trying to carry, and drops its burden. It rejects at last the whole body through the same laws by which it rejects a part of it when that part is spiritually dead.

If you receive with scorn the thought that your physical body through fresher and fresher renewal of Its substance can be made perpetual, you close to yourself an entrance for life, and open another to decay and death.

We do not argue that you "ought" to believe this. You may be so mentally constituted that you cannot now believe it. There are many things to be in the future which none of us have now the power to believe. But we can if the thing deemed impossible be desirable, pray or demand a faith which shall give us a reason for believing, and such faith will come in response to demand.

Faith means power to believe in the true, or the capacity for the mind to receive true thoughts. The faith of Columbus in the existence of a new continent was a power in him to entertain such idea greater than others of his time. People who to use the common expression " have faith in themselves," have also an actual power for carrying our their undertakings greater than those who have no faith in themselves. When you demand faith in possibilities for yourself that now seem new and strange; you demand, also, the power and ability to draw to you the capacity to see or feel reasons for truths new to you. If you demand persistently the truth and only the truth you will get it, and the whole truth means power to accomplish seeming impossibilities.

"Thy faith hath made thee whole" said the Christ of Judea to a man who was healed. To us this passage interprets itself as meaning that the person healed had an innate power of believing that he could be healed. This power which was of his own spirit (and not of Christ's) so acted on his body as instantly to cure his infirmities. Christ was a means of awakening this power in that man's spirit. But Christ himself did not give the person that power. It war latent in the person healed. Christ woke it into life, and probably only temporary life and activity, for we do not hear that any of the recorded cases of sudden healing in those times were permanent. They fell sick again and finally lost their bodies. Why? Because the faith or power they drew to themselves for a brief time did not come to stay. They had not learned to increase it continually through silent demand of the Supreme Power. Their spirits went back into the domain of material belief. When that belief again materialized a load on the spirit hard to carry, and they were sick, not one was at hand like the Christ to awaken it into a temporary faith or power.

No person can become permanently whole (which implies among other powers, immortality in the flesh) and have entire and permanent freedom from disease, who is ever trusting, or leaning on any other save the Supreme to gain the power of faith. In this respect every mind must stand entirely alone. You cannot draw the highest power if you depend always for help from another or others. If you do you are only borrowing or absorbing their faith. Such borrowed faith may work wonders for a time, but it does not come to stay. When that of which you borrow is cut off, you will fall into the slough of despond and disease again. You had really never drawn from the right source—the Supreme.

Our most profitable demand or prayer made consciously or unconsciously is " Let my faith be ever increased."

When you reverse your mental attitude regarding sickness and do but entertain the belief that it is an effort of the spirit to throw off errors in thought which as absorbed and received from earliest infancy are materialized in your flesh, you gradually cease to load up with error. You commence also the process of unloading and casting out all former errors in thought. The sickness you had many years ago in fear of death has in a sense packed away that particular remembrance of such mood of fear in your being, and with it the belief that accompanied such remembrance. That belief has been working against you all these years as all wrong belief must work against you.

It is literally a part of your real being, as all past individual remembrances and experiences are a literal part of our beings. It is retained in your spiritual memory, although its material remembrance may have faded out. That remembrance is in thought a reality. But it is the remembrance of a false belief, teaching that death and decay can never be overcome. This belief, the reversed action and state of your mind will cast out. But such casting out must have a correspondent expression in the flesh. The physical expressions of all your former coughs and colds, fevers and other illness must reappear, at first possibly severe, but gradually in a modified form. You are then unloading your old false beliefs. But if your belief is not reversed and you go on as before, regarding physical decay and death as inevitable, then with every illness in such mental condition you pack away another error, another untruth, and another addition to the load of untruths, whose certain effect, added to the rest, is to weaken, crush, and finally cause the body to perish.

There is no period in the "physical life" too late for receiving or entertaining the truth. There is no period too late for such truth to commence its process of physical renewal, and though that particular physical life may not be perpetuated, yet the spirit in receiving such truth receives a force which will be of priceless value to it on the unseen side, and by its aid it may be able the sooner to build for itself a more perfect spiritual body, and the ultimate of the relatively perfected spiritual body is the power to be and live in the physical and spiritual realms of existence at will.

If you hold to the idea that mankind are always to go on as in the past, losing their bodies, and are also to remain without the power to keep those bodies in perfect health, then you set your belief against the eternal fact that all things in this planet are ever moving forward to greater refinement, greater powers, and greater possibilities.

Medicine and material remedies may greatly assist the throwing-off process. A skilled and sympathetic physician of any school may be of much assistance. Everything depends on the mind and belief in which you take the medicine and the physician's advice. If you regard both as aids to your spirit in throwing off a load and building for you a new body, you give in such belief great help to the spirit, so to throw off and build. But if you regard both medicine and physician as aids only to the body, and a body also which you hold must at best weaken and perish some time during the next thirty, forty or fifty years, you will load up with belief in error faster than you cast it off, and the load becomes at last too heavy for the spirit to carry.

What causes the man or woman to be "bowed down by age?" What causes the stooping shoulders, the weakened knees, the tottering gait? Because they believe only in the earthly and perishable. The spirit is not earthly nor perishable. But you can load it down literally with an earthy quality of thought which will "bow it down toward the earth with such burden."

It is not the physical body of the old person that is bent and bowed down. It is that part which is the force moving the body, that is, his or her spirit loaded with material thought which it cannot appropriate or assimilate, which becomes so bent, bowed and weak. The body is always an external correspondence of your mind or spirit.

A body thus ever renewing, beautifying, freshening and strengthening means a mind behind it ever renewing with new ideas, plans, hope, purpose and aspiration. Life eternal is not the half dead life of extreme old age.

The person who can see only the physical side and temporary expression of life, who eats and drinks in the belief that only the body is affected by less eating and drinking, who believes that the body is sustained only by force, generated within itself, and that it is not fed of an unseen element coming from the spiritual realm of element, and who believes that nothing exists but what he can see, hear and feel with the physical sense (that is the material which is always the temporary and perishable), draws to himself mostly those forces and elements which cause the temporary and perishable, and these acting in his body make it temporary and perishable.

Death of the body begins with thousands many years before they are in their coffins. The pale face, and parchment-coloured skin, means a half dead skin. It means a portion of the body on which the spirit works the casting-out process of dead element, and taking on of the new very imperfectly. In the freshness of infancy and early youth, the spirit cast out and took on more vigorously. As years went on untruth was absorbed by that spirit. Its growth in knowledge was more and more retarded. Responding physical changes became slower and slower. The body commences to show "signs of age," that is to die. Because such spirit was less and less fed of that element which brings constant renewal of new thought which is new life.

So far does the belief and faith in weakness and decay prevail with the race that wisdom is often allegorically portrayed as an old man, gray, baldheaded, bowed and sustained by a staff. That means a wisdom which cannot prevent its own body from falling to pieces. In that form of being we call the child (a spirit or mind having come in possession of a new body), there is for a period a greater spiritual wisdom than when the child is physically more matured. It is the unconscious wisdom of intuition. It is for a time more open to the truth. For such reason, up to the age of eighteen or twenty, the spiritual casting off and taking on processes with the body are more perfectly performed. These relatively rapid changes in the physical maintain the bloom and freshness of youth. Sooner or later, however, the higher spiritual process ceases gradually to operate. Beliefs in the false, as taught or absorbed from others, materialize themselves in the body despite all the resistance of the higher mind as expressed in pain and sickness. The load of belief in the earthy and perishable accumulates. The body assumes an appearance in correspondence with such thought. At last the higher mind refuses longer to carry such a burden, flings it off, and leaves a dead body.

The death of the body is then the final process for casting off cruder element from the spirit which it can no longer use or appropriate. But it is very desirable for the spirit to be able to keep a physical body which shall refine as the spirit refines, because in such equality of refinement between the spirit and its instrument, our increase in happiness is greatly advanced, and the relatively perfected rounding out of our powers cannot be realized until this union between spirit and body is effected.

When the Christ of Judea said to the elders of Israel of the little child, "Except ye become as this child ye cannot enter the Kingdom of Heaven," he meant as the text interprets itself to us, that they should become as open to that inflowing of force as that spirit (the child) was at that period of its existence. Were such influx maintained, the youth of the body would be perpetual.

The child is more "led of the spirit" than the grown-up person. It is more natural. It discards policy. It shows openly whom it likes and whom it does not. It has often more intuition. It will dislike a bad man or a bad woman when its parents see no evil in that person. It knows or rather feels far more regarding life than its parents give it credit for. But it cannot voice its thoughts in words. Yet the thoughts are still there. It has not learned to train itself to the double-faced custom of the world which smiles in your face and sneers behind your back. It is relatively natural. Its spirit for a time gives itself free expression. When the spirit loses this freedom of expression when we pretend what we are not, when we say "Yes" outwardly and think "No" inwardly, when we court only to gain a favour, when we feel anger or disappointment or irritation within and pretend content and happiness without, we become more and more unnatural in all tastes and desires. We blunt and for a time destroy all the higher spiritual senses and powers. We become unable to distinguish truth from falsehood. We are unable to feel spiritually what faith means, much less to draw this great and indispensable power to us, and without this drawing power the physical body must be cast off by the spirit.

The body in dying does not "give up the ghost." It is the ghost (the spirit) that rejects the material body. Its spirit, through casting off unbelief, becomes more and more accessible to thoughts and things that are true, and, therefore, grows to more and more power, it will, acting in all parts and functions of the body, operate the casting-off process more and more quickly, as it does in the material youth. It will refuse or reject through the physical senses of touch or taste anything which would injure or adulterate it. It can attain to such power that an active poison if accidentally placed in the mouth would be instantly detected and rejected, or it swallowed would be instantly cast from the stomach.

It is not the physical stomach which rejects food unfit for it or casts out the nauseous dose. It is the spirit which moves the organ to such action through a knowledge of its own, that the cast-out substance is unfit for it. It is so unfit because there is no spirit nor quality in the rejected element which can assimilate with and help the spirit. As your spirit grows in power this sensitiveness to all things which can do it evil, be they of the seen or unseen world of things, will increase. It grows keener and keener to the approach or presence of everything evil, and casts it off. It will warn you instantly of the evil or designing person. It will tell you what is safe and fit for your association. It will at last cast out or refuse to receive all evil thoughts which now you may daily receive unconsciously, and which work more harm than anything material can do, for by them the spirit is poisoned.

As faith increases many material aids will be called in by the spirit which will greatly help the renewing processes. These aids will come in the selection of foods, in choosing proper associations and other changes of habit and custom. But it is the spirit which must prompt and direct these material aids. When such prompting comes you will be obliged to follow it. The food to be avoided, you will not be able to eat. Your taste will reject it. The association injurious to you, you will not be able to keep company with. The habit to be changed will drop off easily and naturally.

But if you make any rigid rules for yourself in these matters in the hope they will tend to spiritualize you, you are allowing the material self to take the matter in hand. The material or lower mind is then trying to give the law and rule and refine the spiritual or higher self. Let the spirit increased in faith, do the work, and when the time comes for you to reject any animal food or any of the grosser element in any form, the desire and relish for these will have gone.

In stating our belief that immortality in the flesh is a possibility, we do not infer that it is one which any now, physically alive, may realize. Neither do we infer it is one they cannot realize. Nor do we argue that people should immediately set to work in any material sense in order to "live forever." We hold only that it is one result which must come sooner or later of that spirit evolution or growth from the cruder to the finer, which has always been operating on this planet and on every form of matter. Matter is spirit temporarily materialized so as to be evident to correspondent physical sense.

As we grow in the faith of these spiritual processes for casting out the old and taking in the new, and consequently realize the accompanying greater refinement or spiritualization of the body, we shall aid more and more those who are nearest us in the unseen side of life. For as we become more spiritualized in the flesh they are helped to materialize more of the spirit. In other words, we shall become physically tangible each to the other, because in the material thought we cast off there exists an element which they can appropriate to make themselves more material. Their spiritual bodies are also under the same laws as regards the throwing off and taking-on process. What they throw off as coarser to them is the finer and fit for us, This element we spiritually absorb. It is for the time and condition a certain spiritual food and life for us. Through what they throw off we are aided to spiritualize the body. Through what we throw off they are aided to materialize the spirit.

The Attraction of Aspiration

Why may we not maintain a level of serenity of mind? Why are we so subject to periods of depression?

It is because, no matter how well-positioned you are in accord with your ideal of living, you are still to a greater or less degree affected by the discordance which reigns about you. Are you gentle and humane toward the animal creation? The wild birds, your free pets who come and build their nests in the grove, are murdered for sport or gain before your eyes and you are quite helpless to prevent it. You live amid a scene of incessant cruelty and slaughter. The animals fostered by man's care are bred under artificial conditions and thereby developed into unnatural and really unhealthy growths for his amusement or profit. This refers to all manner of "fancy breeding." Nature when left alone does best for bird or animal, and the birds or animals have their individual rights as well as man. A strained and morbid taste will grow an enlarged and diseased liver in a goose to make thereof a certain dish. Your race are so growing disease all about you. Disease means mental as well as physical unhappiness. Directly and indirectly this unhappiness affects you.

The finer your organization and the more open is it to a finer life, the more easily annoyed is it here by the many ills about it. You can hardly go abroad without suffering mental or physical pain. Your houses, cars and boats in winter are overheated and full of noxious vapours from the fuel used, as well as emanation from the human bodies packed in them. You may be obliged to sleep in rooms where this unhealthy heat is partly relied on to warm your when at rest. You must breathe it when in the unconscious state of recuperation, and awake with it incorporated into your being. You are liable to eat staleness and decay at the best of your public tables. You are pained by scenes of cruelty, brutality and injustice. That is the predominant thought active in the atmosphere of the crowd, and it affects your thought.

There is thought, or if you please so to call it, mental action embodied in every material thing about you, and the brightness or darkness of the thought depends on the condition of the material thing. The eating of stale fruit or vegetables may indirectly give you the blues. The live fresh fruit gives you life. Decay is the disorganization of matter. You want to feed on the perfect organization, neither over nor under ripe. You want it, if possible, when the article fed upon is at its fullest stage of life, so that you may receive that life.

You violate ignorantly, unconsciously, and even for the time, necessarily, many laws of physical and mental health. Relative to food, air, warmth, as spoken of above, you may always have been dependent on artificial props. You were born so dependent. You may have come into the world with a body, the partial development of artificial and improper food, and an artificial life brought down to you through the blood of many generations.

This artificial life must in some way bring pain. Your alcoholic stimulant brightens for the moment but leaves a much longer period of pain behind it. But the evil of alcohol is really small as compared with scores of causes for human ills in daily active operation about you in places crowded with people, and all the more dangerous from being quite unknown.

You ask, why even in solitude you cannot maintain a certain evenness and serenity of mind of which you realize sufficient to long for?

Assuming that in the past you have been diseased physically, and of course mentally, do you expect to be instantly cured of such a long illness? Certain habits of thought cannot be otherwise than gradually removed. So with certain habits of body consequent on such habits of thought, such as the habit of hurry, the habit of worry, the habit of laying undue stress on things not the most needful for the hour; the habit of trouble borrowing and many others, which permeate and influence every act of life. Their combined effect is exhaustion, and exhaustion is the real mother of most of the ills flesh is heir to.

Whatever exhausts the body, be the motive for effort of good or ill, benevolence or selfishness, lessens the power to resist these many causes for pain and consequent depression of spirits.

So long as earthiness or grosser spirit has the ascendancy, we see mostly on the earth side. We sense mostly the repulsive in the individual. We are slow to see the good. We can like but few. We dislike many. But when spirit gains the ascendancy, this is reversed. We see then clearly the good in all. We are thereby attracted more or less to all. And as we find the good in all, we get good, from all. We cease then to be so strongly repelled by individual prejudices. We love more than we hate. While earthiness prevails we hate more than we love. We see more to loathe and detest than to admire. We are blinded to the good and too sensitive to the evil. Seeing and feeling then more of evil than good, we are injured by it. To hate, to be strongly prejudiced, to be unable to hear mention of the loathed person's name without a thrill of indignation or disgust, is to be continually inflicting wounds on self. To be able to admire, to have the clear sight to detect the good in the lowest nature and to keep the evil out of sight, is a source to us of strength, of health, of continual increase of power. Love is power. You are always the stronger when In a condition of admiration.

Attraction is the Law of Heaven, repulsion that of Earth. Spirituality is attracted to what it finds of itself anywhere. It sees the diamond in the rough, though embedded in the coarsest mould. It sees the germ of superior quality in the coarsest nature. It can fix its eye on that germ, and hide from itself the coarser elements. In so doing it throws its power on that germ, and warms it into life. The basest nature mounts to its highest level in the presence and under the influence of the higher. There is little need for the true missionary to preach in words. He or she exhales an atmosphere of divinity which is felt by all. Precepts need to be felt more than heard. The prejudiced against the sinner is only a spiritual porcupine. He stings all he touches.

So long as we feel that strong repulsion, through seeing only the defects in another, so long are we ruled by such sentiment. We are in fetters. We are in his or her presence so full of hatred as to be unable to assert the better part of ourselves. All our own evil is called out and comes to the front. There is only the clashing of opposing wills. In such case, we, though in reality the more powerful party, become the weaker for the time being. We are obliged to allow the pupil whom we should teach by example to domineer over us. Cynicism is born of repulsion and personal prejudice carried to its extreme. The cynic ends by finding everybody unbearable and at last hates himself. No cynic was ever in good health. Cynicism is blood poisoning. The cynic is ever hunting for the ideal without. He should find it within. This when once found would be ever creating ideals from all without. His own loving spirit would graft and build itself or all with whom he came in contact.

Divinity is also contagious. That would be a poor Divine Plan which allowed only evil to be infectious. Goodness is catching. In good time the world will learn that health is also. But hitherto mankind have so much feared and even admired the devil, as to have accredited evil only with inoculating quality, while all manner of good is supposed to be drilled into poor human nature by painful and laborious processes.

There cannot be the highest health and vigour without aspiration and purity of thought. Pure thought brings the purest blood. Impure thought, despondent, hopeless, repining, fault-finding, fretful slanderous thought is certain to make the blood impure and fill the system with disease. Without aspiration your best care for the body will be relatively of little help. You may as to garb and person be scrupulously clean; you may pay the utmost attention to diet; yet after all you are but cleaning the outside of a vessel which within is ever filling up with uncleanliness.

With an ever increasing purity of thought, cleanliness and care for the body will come as a natural result. The vessel will clean itself. Proper care for the body in all respects will be a loving effort for that body. Bathing will not be an enforced task but a recreation. Diet will be regulated by the natural demand of appetite. Taste or relish will be the standard for acceptance or rejection. Excess will be impossible, so watchful will be the healthy palate to regard the first faint sign of sufficiency as the signal to cease any kind of indulgence. It is this aspiration for the highest and best that in time causes an actual new birth of the body—a total "reformation" throughout in the quality and composition of flesh, bone, blood, muscle and sinews; a change in the material organization corresponding with that of the spiritual. The flesh by it is spiritualized, that is, made up of finer elements. In all aspiring minds is this process going on. The rule of spirit over flesh brings perfect immunity from disease, intensifies every power, gives far greater capacity for effort in any field, and at the close of the Earth life ensures a painless passing out of the spirit—a simple falling to sleep of the earthly body and a waking up on the other, the spiritual side of life.

The path of self-healing lies in the calling for the elements of health and strength, to drive out disease. That is you pray for such elements and they come to you. Strength or vigour is an element of spirit or more refined matter. The more often is your will exercised in praying for it, the quicker will it come. This is the secret for the perpetual maintenance and increase of vigour or any other desired quality. When sensible—by signs quickly detected—of lack of power, call, pray, desire more. Its rapport with the elements causes such power immediately to flow in upon it. You may become weary. Your will put thus in operation causes an immediate influx of strength, as soon as it places itself in certain conditions for such inflowing.

Say you arise in the morning weak, languid, with no physical or mental energy. Keep your mind as much as you can from dwelling on your ailment. Keep it as much as you can on the thought of strength, vigour, health, activity. As aids to erect this frame of mind, fix it as much as you can on illustrations and symbols of Nature's force and power, on storm and tempest, on the heaving billow and majesty of the Ocean, on the Morning Sun rising in all his glory to refresh and invigorate man, animal and vegetation. If there be in prose or poetry any illustrations of this character which affect you strongly, recur to them. Read them, aloud or in silence. Because in so doing you are setting the mind in the right direction to receive strength. In brief think of strength and power and you will draw it to you. Think of health and you get it. Let your mind dwell on weakness, on never getting well, on the dark side, on everything of discouragement, gloom and darkness and you draw to you the contrary and hurtful elements.

As decay attracts and generates decay in the things we see, so does any weak decaying order of thought attract its like of the things we do not see. Unconsciously many sick and ailing people nurse their complaints more than they nurse the bodies carrying such complaints. They are always thinking of them and talking of them. They actually crave sympathy for the hurt more than for the body afflicted with it. And the sympathy so brought out from surrounding friends, actually nourishes the injury and increases the ailment, when the thought of patient and friends should be placed on a strong healthy body for the patient. The more of such thought concentrated on the patient from those about him or her, the more of drawing power you have to bring vigour to the one afflicted.

Bear in mind it is not here argued that such relief can always be immediate. A mind long unconsciously set in the opposite direction of dwelling on self weakness, cannot immediately reverse its movement and set itself in the contrary and strength-drawing direction. It may have become so habituated and trained to dwell on the dark side as to be almost unable to fix itself on any other. But as the attempt is made and persisted in, more and more power will come to put it in the desired strength attracting frame. The effort must be made. It may take time, but every atom of effort so made is an accretion of strength which can never be lost.

Do not demand arbitrarily or despotically that any member of your body get well of a hurt, that any organ or function become stronger. Your body is as a whole an individual separate from your spirit and with a peculiar physical life of its own, as a whole it is an organization made up of a number of other organizations, each charged with a specific duty, as the eye to see, the ear to hear, the tongue to taste, the stomach to digest, the lungs to breathe. All of these are in a sense individual organizations. Each is open to the enlivening, cheering effect upon it of the element called " love" and that element you can send it. Bandage a hurt, lovingly, tenderly and the element not only inspires the careful, tender treatment, but it goes into the hurt. It acts as a salve and a strength. It gradually binds and unites the ruptured parts. Bind it with indifference, bind or wash it as an irksome task and the sentiment inspires not only a careless and even rough treatment, but fails so to salve and strengthen it with the needed element—love. Bind it with actual hatred and you are self-poisoning the part affected. Hate is the element of poison, Love of healing.

The same principle and process applies to the weak eye, the deafened ear or any ailing or weak organ. Will at times your affection direct to the ailing member, and in that spirit ask it to recover its strength. Be not deterred by the apparent simplicity of this statement, but try it. If you are impatient or angry at eye, or ear, for not being perfect in their office, you do but throw that element of impatience on those organs. You fret and annoy them in their efforts to do their best. There is as yet no such thing as a relatively perfected life among our race. Because such a life means a life and a body without disease or pain, and also a life without the present form of death to the body. A relatively perfected life means a life whereby a mind or spirit has grown to, or gathered so much power by simply asking or praying for power; or in other words, setting that mind as a magnet in the proper attitude to attract power, that it shall be able constantly to recuperate or make over the body with fresher, newer and finer material, and also to put this body on or take it off, materialize it at pleasure, as did the Christ immediately after his crucifixion. The Jews had only destroyed his material body. The spirit of Christ had power to re-clothe itself with a new body. Of this another record illustration is the prophet Elijah's translation to Heaven. That which his companion Elisha saw was Elijah's spiritual or finer body, the counterpart of his material body, and this body was of such fine element that it had come into the domain of and could make use of an attraction not yet recognized by our scientists—the attraction or power which draws upward the opposite of the attraction of gravitation which draws downward or toward the earth. The Attraction of Aspiration.

Every thought or desire of ours to be nobler, more refined, more free from malice, ill-will to others, and to do others good without exacting conditions is a thing, a force of unseen element which does actually tend or draw upward, or in other words, away from the earth or any form of that cruder type of spirit seen of the physical eye, or apparent to the body's touch which we call matter. This the aspiring order of thought you draw from the higher realms of spirit or element every time you wish, pray, or desire it. You are drawing to you then, that of unseen element which incorporates itself with your body and spirit, and it then commences literally to draw you toward the realm and element of greater, broader, purer life existent in zones or bands about our planet. It will, as you persist in this aspiring thought, make you stand more erect. The phrase "the upright man" or woman implies that the effect of this unseen element so brought you of aspiration makes you physically as well as spiritually upright. It lifts every physical organ into place. It is the thought current drawing from above the mood of impure or immature thoughts the mood of unwise or personal selfishness which seeks only personal gratification without thought or care of others. The thought or mood of gloom, discouragement, self depreciation comes of the the overruling attraction of earthly seen or physical things.

When you are ruled by the attraction of gravitation, or, in other words, the attraction of material things, it will tend to make your shoulders rounded he and stooping, your head bowed and your eye down- cast. Your heart will also in some way be literally bowed down through grief, or worry, or anger, or some form of immature thought or attraction coming of seen things or cruder forms of spirit. Every organ of the body will be similarly displaced and tend toward the earth. There is always between things and forms material and things and forms spiritual, an exact and literal correspondence. The shape of every man and woman's body, the expression of the face, their every gesture and mannerism to the crook of a finger, and their physical health, is an exact correspondence of their spiritual condition or, in other words, of the state of their minds. It is a duplication in seen matter and movement of what they are thinking in unseen matter.

As you are ruled more and more by the attraction of aspiration, the desire to be more and more of a God or Goddess, the determination to conquer all the evil within you, which is the only way to conquer any and all evil outside of you, your form will in accordance grow more upright, your eye will be more open and uplifted, your heart will be "lifted up," your cheeks will bloom with fresher colour, your blood will fill more and more with a finer and powerful element, giving to your limbs strength, vigour, suppleness and elasticity of movement. You are then filling more and more with the Elixir of Life, which is no myth but a spiritual reality and possibility.

Our race hitherto has been dominated by the attraction of physical things or seen element. It has said there is nothing in existence but what can be seen or felt of the outer inferior or coarser senses, and consequently there has been nothing else to us. A man may perish of thirst surrounded by springs of cool water, and if he know not of such springs there are none for him. Our condition has been analogous to that.

With the more perfected race of the future on this planet there will be no painful death of the body as at present. Every such painful death is the direct result of sin and transgression of the Law of Life. The ending of the body of the future will be the birth or development of a new physical body for which the old one shall serve as a shell or envelope until the new one is ripe and ready to come forth in a manner analogous to the development of the moth or butterfly from the cocoon. Such growths and transitions will take place at lesser and lesser intervals, until at last the spirit will grow to such power that it can will and attract to itself instantly out of surrounding elements a body to use so long as it pleases on this stratum of life This is the condition foreseen by Paul when he said, "O Death, where is thy sting? O grave, where is thy victory?" And again where he writes, "The last great enemy which shall be overcome is Death." We quote Paul, because no ancient teacher has more plainly foreshadowed these possibilities than he. Undoubtedly they were known to others both of the recorded and unrecorded human history of this planet which stretches back to periods far more remote than those inferred in the Mosaic creation.

These truths, these possibilities for avoiding decay, death and pain, and growing into and taking on a newer and newer body, and newer, fresher and more vigorous life, vitally affect us of today. We must not regard these statements as affecting only a coming race of people of some far distant future They affect us. They are possibilities for us. We have belonging to us the powers for bringing to us new rife and new bodies. If you are not told of these your powers how can you ever use them? You are then as a pauper having, unknown to yourself, a thousand dollar bank note sewed up in the lining of your ragged coat. This knowledge is for you the "pearl of great price." You cannot sell this pearl. You cannot trade it for that of your neighbour's. You cannot accumulate your neighbour's powers; you can only grow and use yours alone.

You wonder perhaps and say, "Can these truths, these marvels belong to our common-place age and time? "But ours is not a common-place, or prosaic age and time. It is only our lack of seeing clearly which may make our time seem common-place. We live surrounded by the same elements, and we are in possession of the same powers to greater or lesser extent, whereby the three young Jews passed unharmed through the fiery fumace—whereby the Prophet Daniel, through exercise of the superior force of human thought, quelled the ferocity of the lions in the den; whereby Paul shook off the serpent's venom; whereby the Man of Nazareth performed his wonderful works. " Was not this God's power?" you ask. Yes, the power of God or the Infinite and incomprehensible spirit of Eternal Good working in and through these His children, as the same power can work in and through us the more we call it to us, demand it, importune it and depend upon it. It is simply the power of the higher mind over the lower or cruder mind. All seen element, or as we call it matter, is expression of the lower or cruder mind. Rocks, hills, clouds, waves, trees, animals and men, are all varying expressions of the lower cruder mind. The power of mind over matter means the power of the higher mind over all these expressions of the lower mind.

The aspiration, the earnest prayer or demand to be better, to have more power, to become more refined, will bring more and more of the finer elements and forces; that is spirit to you. But the motive must be the natural heart-felt zealous wish to impart what you receive to others. You cannot call the fullness of this power to you if you intend living only for self. You may get it to a degree and accomplish much by it. Your demand if living only for self may bring to you houses, wealth and fame. But the demand based on the selfish motive will in the end bring only pain, disease and disappointment.

The Accession of New Thought

New thought is new life. When an invention, a discovery first breaks on the inventor's mind, it fills him with joy. The blood in his veins surges with a fresher impetus. The author or poet is lifted into ecstasy of emotion by a new conception; I mean the relatively few creative authors and poets—not the many who, borrowing the fire of Genius, put it in their own lanterns and pass it off, often successfully as their own.

"A piece of good news," as we term it in a period of gloom, depression, discouragement; the possible realization of a hope, the removal of an ill or danger, is but a thought after all—is but the picture in the mind of the thing desired—is not the thing itself, yet how it brings strength to the whole body.

An entertaining spectacle, a drama so perfectly acted as to absorb all one's attention, an interview with one to whom we are strongly attracted, a pursuit, or exercise, or art, which interests and fascinates—all these are as food and nourishment, stimulation to the body, and in the absorbtion or excitement of the moment, hunger for material food may pass away or be forgotten.

So we do not live by bread alone. But our natures demand ever new and newer food of thought. The play so charming when first seen may become tiresome through repetition. The air so fascinating when first heard, becomes worn through familiarity. There may even be longed for, a change from the quality of the thought of the mind most attractive to us.

I mean for all these a change, but only for a time. The play, the opera, the artist may in time be seen again and with increase of pleasure, either from the influence of former association, or from new growths and shadings in the artist's rendering, or from new capacity in ourselves to see what we could not see before. Call, then, all new thought, and if you please new emotion, food—food as necessary to make the relatively perfect physical and mental man or woman as is the bread we eat. We desire ever fresh food; we similarly desire and need always new and fresh thought.

Old thought—constant repetition of the same thought—involves decay, sluggishness of mind, sluggishness of body.

Suppose that we rose each morn with the absolute certainty that each day was to be a day involving to us more or less of the excitement of discovery in something useful and enjoyable, and also of similar use to others—something endurable for us and others—endurable for eternity—some unexpected branching out of yesterday's truth, which for yesterday seemed fully grown—something telling us how life may be made still fuller of durable and harmless enjoyment; some great law principle in Nature recognized possibly for the first time in some heretofore called "little thing," in the fall of a leaf, in the colouring of a leaf by the autumnal frost, in its almost equal vividness of colour coming through the heat of Spring.

What must be the pleasure to an open and receptive mind to find today an increase of improvement in the quality almost despaired of yesterday—an increase of patience in doing the perplexing work —an increase of courage—an increase of perception to see beauty in what yesterday it passed by with indifference—an increase of power to control unruly appetite—an increase of power to drive away unpleasant and therefore injurious thought.

Would not such be encouraging, cheering, life giving, health-giving thoughts? This order and accession of ever new thought knows no stop in any direction. It says: "Are you orderly today? You will find some power and room and capacity to be more orderly tomorrow. "Was your last effort in music, in painting, in composition, in acting, in oratory, your greatest triumph?" "You will find some way of making it more perfect tomorrow." That will take nothing from the last effort. It is only a more beautiful and delicate tint for some already beautiful picture. The consciousness of such never-ending growth of improvement is also food for the growing mind, other than bread. Yet it is bread. It is the "Bread of Life," and to be desired as "Our Daily Bread."

Would not also the thought each morning that a Great Power, an infinitely wise mind, was always ready to give more knowledge to help you through troubles—troubles from without and troubles from within. Would not such thought, and the trust begotten of it, be as food, strength, and healthy stimulation?

Especially when the reality of this Power and its ability to aid had been proven to you many times, so that the hope had become a conviction? Grant that new thought is healthy stimulation and also a necessary food to a more perfected life and the question arrives, "How shall we get it?" In other words, "How may we attune ourselves or how may we become more receptive to all that is beautiful and useful in Nature?" For in our religion the useful always implies the beautiful. It is almost farcical to answer, "Live a pure life." That implies so much; so much in so many cases to be done; so much of inherent tendency to be outgrown; so many difficulties to be met; so many conditions necessary for such life so difficult to make. The desire for accumulation seems a Law of our Natures. In its cruder working it accumulates money: in its higher form it would accumulate powers and qualities of mind. "I am $100 or $500 richer than I was this morning," says, with satisfaction and pleasure at night, the money accumulator. That pleasant thought is to him a bit of the bread of Life—but not of enduring life, or in the end, if at all healthy life.

"I," may say another man at night, "am richer than I was this morning by so much more patience, by a bit more of skill or dexterity in my art, by certain knowledge of which I knew nothing twenty four hours ago."

Are we yet fully awakened to the thought that we are receptacles for thought and with thought knowledge, and with knowledge Power, and that our capacity for receiving all these may be limitless, and that the supply of knowledge, power, new thought in the Universe is limitless also, and that it is all ours to draw from, and that the Bank can no more break than Eternity can end.

There are thousands of things, events and scenes in your past life which it is more profitable to forget than to remember. By so forgetting you allow entrance for new idea, which is new life. By remembering you prevent the coming to you of such new idea and life.

By "forgetting," I mean that you should avoid living in unpleasant past scenes and remembrances. Absolutely to forget or wipe out completely from memory anything it has once taken note of is impossible. For everything you have seen, learned, sensed or heard is stored away, and is capable under certain circumstances of being brought to view again.

In place of the term forgetting it would be better to say you should cultivate the power of driving from your mind and putting out of sight whatever makes you feel unhappy or whatever you discover that is unprofitable to remember.

It is impossible absolutely to wipe out anything your memory has once written on its tablets, for whatever the scene, event or experience may have been, it has become a part of your real self or spirit. In other words your spirit is made up of all its experiences and consequent remembrances extending to an infinite past. Of these some are vivid, some vague, and much is buried out of present sight, but capable under certain circumstances of being called to remembrance. To destroy such remembrance, if possible, would be to destroy so much of your mind.

All experiences are valuable for the wisdom they bring or suggest. But when you have once gained wisdom and knowledge from any experience, there is little profit in repeating it, especially if it has been unpleasant, You do actually repeat it when you remember it or live it over again in thought. This is what people are doing who brood over past misfortunes and disappointments.

It is what people are doing when they recall with regret their youth as bright and joyous as compared with the gloom of their middle or old age. Live in the pleasant remembrance of your youth, if you so desire. That will do you good. But do not set it in its brightness and freshness against a dark background of the present. Do not think of it in that vein.

Remember that the time of your infancy and youth, with all its freshness and newness, was also the time of some other people's old age when the world seemed stale and joyless, when to them all that life seemed capable of yielding seemed exhausted, when nothing seemed to remain but to wither and die. Remember also that today if the world seems less bright than formerly, if the sun seems setting instead of rising, it seems now to the boy and girl of ten or fifteen as it did to you at that age.

No person could hold his or her physical body and enjoy life who as they lived on lived in the past and refused to set or open their minds to the future. In so doing they accumulate more and more of the old and relatively lifeless thought, and this element materializes itself on the body. Their flesh, bone and blood then become an actual expression of the dead and inert spirit.

To live carrying such an ever-increasing load must result only in weakness and misery so long as the spirit can carry it. But the mind rejecting the old which it has no use for and ever pressing on to the new, adds the new thought to itself, and this newness of idea will materialize a newer body.

You do actually make the "things before " pleasant or unpleasant for you according as you think of them in advance.

There is a class of people who, if in difficulties and anyone suggests a way out, instantly raise objections and find difficulties in the plan proposed. When in thought we so find difficulties, we actually make them. To lay awake nights and brood, devise, turn over or invent possible coming troubles is force and industry ill employed in preparing the way for those troubles.

In all business we must press on in mind to the successful result. We must see in mind or imagination the thing we plan completed, the system or method organized and in working order, the movement or undertaking advancing and ever growing stronger and more profitable. To spend time and force in looking back and living past troubles or obstacles over again, and out of such living and mental action to conjure more difficulties or oppositions, is literally to spend time and force in destroying your undertaking, or in manufacturing obstacles to put in your own way.

Forgetting the things behind and pressing on to those before is a maxim having a thousand intensely practical applications. Every business success is founded on it.

Men who cease to live in old methods and press forward to new, achieve the greatest financial success. But men who having started out during their physical youth with the new, allow themselves with advancing years to hold on to what was new in their youth, but which is relatively old now, are really on the back track. Money may continue to pour in upon them, but their methods are really out of date, and a few more years will see their business superseded by the newer system.

If you were debilitated, weak or sick yesterday at any hour, do not commence today with living in thought in the same weakness or debility at that hour. Forget it, live away from it, and press onward to the thought of being strong, well and vigorous at that hour.

When you in mind look behind and live behind the thought of the sickness, weakness or indisposition of yesterday, you are actually making the conditions for having the same physical troubles. When you at the day's commencement in thought look before to the new thing, the thought of health and strength at the time your lack of vigour commenced, you are making the conditions for realizing such health and strength.

If it does not come the first day of such trial, try the next, and the next after that. The state you seek will come in time.

Perhaps you say to me in mind: But how can you prove these assertions? They have not been realized in our time. "Decay and death at last overtake all"

You can commence yourself to prove them. If you experiment with any of the methods here suggested for working thought to profitable result and you prove for yourself ever so little, you must thereby gain some faith in this law. If the law is by you proven a little, is it unreasonable to say it will prove more if followed in this direction?

Unreasoning prejudices are bred out of this continual living in the past. The man of sixty or seventy often lives in moods, usages and customs peculiar to his youth. He accepts these as the most fit and proper thing for him. He would probably regard with disfavour and prejudice the man who at his daily business should wear the knee breeches, stockings, waistcoat, ruffled shirt and cocked hat of the eighteenth century. Yet such style was common one hundred years ago. His great-grandfather probably wore such a suit. Yet his great-grandfather would probably have regarded with the same disfavour and prejudice the man dressed in the fashion of today. So a few years relatively have begotten these two unreasoning prejudices with the great-grandfather and great-grandson, founded only on the fact that they were fashions peculiar to the youth of each.

It is, of course, impossible for a person to fly in the face of popular custom or usage—to dress differently or in certain ways live differently without bringing on him unpleasant and even injurious results. For the action of many minds sending toward you ever the thought of prejudice, dislike or ridicule would tend to injure mind and body.

But the sentiment which sends this kind of thought toward another, who departs from any established custom, when that person thereby affects no one's peace or comfort, is a gross error. It is an unreasoning mental tyranny which so regards with hostile mind a man who, e.g., should today adopt the costume of the ancient Greeks—a garb, by the way, more sensible and comfortable than ours.

Less than two hundred years ago such a sentiment mobbed the man in England who carried the first umbrella. This sentiment comes of that fossilized condition of mind which persists in living in the things that are behind and averts itself from such as are before.

Life is a continual advance forward. If we are advancing forward, it is better to look forward. And all are advancing, even the dullest, the grossest, and most perverse. A mighty, eternal and incomprehensible force pushes us all forward. But while all are so being pushed, many linger and look back. Unconsciously, they oppose this force. So to do is to court evil, pain, disease and distress.

Whatever the mind is set upon, or whatever it keeps most in view, that it is bringing to it, and the continual thought or imagining must at last take form and shape in the world of seen and tangible things.

I repeat this assertion often in these books and in various forms of expression because this fact is the cornerstone of your happiness or misery, permanent health and prosperity, or poverty. It needs to be kept as much as possible in mind. Our thought is the unseen magnet, ever attracting its correspondence in things seen and tangible. As we realize this more and more clearly, we shall become more and more careful to keep our minds set in the right direction. We shall be more and more careful to think happiness and success instead of misery and failure. It is very wonderful that the happiness or misery of our lives should be based on what seems so simple a law and method. But so-called "simple" things in Nature on investigation generally turn out incomprehensible and ever deepening mysteries. What most concerns us is to know a cause or agency that will produce a given result. When we realize that we can and do think ourselves into what we are, as regards health, wealth and position, we realize also that we have found in ourselves "the pearl of great price," and we hasten to tell our neighbour that he may seek and find in himself this pearl and power also, for no one is made poorer through his finding that which can belong to him alone, and all are made richer and happier as each finds his or her pearl, through the power it gives them to add to the general wealth and happiness.

Life is fuller of possibilities for pleasure than has ever been realized. The real life means a perpetual and ever increasing maturity. It means the preservation of the physical body, so that it can be used on this stratum of existence whenever the spirit desires to use it. It means the preservation of that body, not only free from pain and sickness, but free from the debility, weakness and decay of what we call "old age," which is in reality only the wearing out of the instrument used by the spirit for lack of knowledge to ever recuperate and regenerate it.

Life means the development in us of powers and pleasures which fiction in its highest flights has never touched. It means an ever-increasing freshness, an ever-increasing perception and realization of all that is grand, wonderful and beautiful in the universe, a constantly increasing discovery of more and more that is grand, beautiful and wonderful, and a constantly increasing capacity for the emotional part of our natures to sense such happiness. Life is eternal in the discovery and realization of these joys. Their source is inexhaustible. Their quality and character must be unknown until they reach us. In the words of the Apostolic record, "Eye hath not seen nor ear heard, neither have entered into the heart of man the things which God hath prepared for them that love Him."

In so-called ordinary things we get out of our lives and our senses but the merest fragment of the pleasure they can be made capable of giving us. Our food is capable of giving far more pleasure to the sense of taste than it may now. We do not get nearly as much pleasure from the ear and eye as they are capable of giving. With bodies more highly developed and refined, food when taken into the stomach should act as a healthy stimulant and give that impulse, vigour and bounding life which it gives to the young animal. The movement of every muscle, as in walking, can be made to give pleasure.

Through following the Spiritual Law, that peace of mind "which passeth all understanding" is in the future to come to many. That it has not in the past been realized is no proof it will not be. Life, then, whether its forces are in activity or at rest, will ne perpetual Elysium.

But millions of our race do not look forward to such joyous possibilities at all. They have never heard of them. The great majority would not believe did they hear of them. They press on in mind to what?

To a belief which grows stronger with years that life is short, that old age and decay are absolute certainties and must come to all, that at a certain age of the body its powers must decrease, and that as weak and feeble old men and women now are before their eyes, so, in time, they must be, and that one great aim of life should be to lay up a store of money to "provide for old age."

These are not pleasant things to contemplate. The many do not contemplate them. They shut their eyes to these gloomy views of their future, but they believe in them just the same. They believe and dread. If they believe, they must in mind press on to such belief. It is this pressing forward that makes of the thing believed in, a material or physical reality.

"Providing for old age" makes the old age of the body, because the person so "providing" sees him or herself for years as helpless and decrepit. What the mind so projects for the future it is making for the future. A material thing (money) is relied on to secure one from ills, when all material things are quite powerless to prevent such ills. The rich man with an aged, worn, diseased body can only buy with his money a better room and bed to live in than the poor man. His money does not prevent disease and weakness. It cannot give him an appetite for the costliest food. In pain and anguish the Emperor is in all respects on the same level with the pauper, for in extreme misery a soft bed and numerous attendants give little or no comfort.

Now in all this, thought element worked in ignorance in the wrong direction proves that it brings a result, but a woeful one. It is only the cultivation of the power of the spirit over the body that can prevent these ills. That power we first begin to cultivate and increase when we come to recognize and believe that mind or spirit is the power governing our bodies, and that whatever mind persistently images, thinks or imagines, it makes. Now, unconsciously, we image in the wrong direction. We think the old age or wearing out of the body must be, because, so far as we know, it always has been. We press on in imagination and unwelcome belief to gloom and physical decay. We hold these sad pictures ever in our minds. Having no faith in the brighter view, we do not look toward that view to life, and ever increasing life.

In the New Testament (the last revelation) we find the Christian and Apostolic teaching full of the sentiment of life, and life everlasting. Death is not argued or implied as an absolute necessity, but as an "enemy" which is ultimately to be destroyed.

It was never said or implied that the advent of "greater revelations" was not to be until millions on millions of years in the future. The dawn of such advent may be now. It is now, not because of any one man's writings or assertions, but because many minds are now open to the reception of the greater revelation, which for centuries has been knocking at humanity's door, but could not enter by reason of the obtuseness and dull ear of those whom it sought to arouse and benefit.

The only dead people in the Universe are the spiritually dead, those "dead in trespasses and sins" who have not as yet learned to forget or rather to refuse to live in and depend on the relatively dead or inert element of earth instead of that drawn from a higher source.

Still the few in the vanguard pressing onward are crying out: "Why, here under our noses is the greatest of all motive powers! Why, human thought is a real element, a real force, darting out like electricity from every man's or woman's mind, injuring or relieving, killing or curing, building fortunes or tearing them down, working for good or ill, every moment, night or day, asleep or awake, carving, moulding and shaping people's faces and making them ugly or agreeable.

Before you give so much of your thought to others, ask. in view of these possibilities, if some is not due to yourself. If you can build yourself up into a living power—if you can, with others, prove that physical health and vigour can take the place of old age—that all disease can be banished from the body—that material riches and necessities can come of laws and methods not now generally practised, and that life is not the short, unsatisfactory, hopeless thing which at the best it now is, will you not to the world at large do a thousand-fold more good than if you expended your thought in feeding a few hungry mouths or relieving a few physical necessities of others?

Our richest men, our rulers, our famous men in art, science and war, our professors, our ministers, our greatest successes, what is their end? Weakness decay and disease. Our more thoughtful people admit that by the time they have learned something of life, it is time to die. The obituary from the living is at best an apology for the unsatisfactory ending of a human life.

Mankind demand something better. That demand, that cry has been swelling and increasing in volume for many centuries. Demand must always be answered. This demand is now being answered, first to the few, next to the many. New light, new knowledge and new results in human life and all it involves, are coming to this earth.

The God in You

CONTENTS

Positive and Negative Thought

Your mind or spirit is continually giving out its force or thought, or receiving some quality of such force, as an electric battery may be sending out its energy and may be afterwards replenished. When you use your force in talking, or writing, or physical effort of any sort, you are positive. When not so using it, you are negative. When negative, or receptive, you are receiving force or element of some kind or quality, which may do you temporary harm or permanent good.

All evil of any kind is but temporary. Your spirit's course through all successive lives is toward the condition of ever-increasing and illimitable happiness.

There are poisonous atmospheres of thought as real as the poisonous fumes of arsenic or other metallic vapors. You may, if negative, in a single hour, by sitting in a room with persons whose minds are full of envy, jealousy, cynicism or despondency, absorb from them a literally poisonous element of thought, full of disease. It is as real as any noxious gas, vapor or miasma. It is infinitely more dangerous, so subtle is its working, for the full injury may not be realized till days afterwards, and is then attributed to some other cause.

It is of the greatest importance where you are, or by what element of thought, emanating from other minds, you are surrounded when in the negative or receiving state. You are then as a sponge, unconsciously absorbing element, which may do great temporary harm or great permanent good to both mind and body.

During several hours of effort of any kind, such as talking business, walking, writing, or superintending your household, or doing any kind of artistic work, you have been positive, or sending out force. You have then to an extent drained yourself of force. If now you go immediately to a store crowded with hurried customers, or to a sick person, or a hospital, or a turbulent meeting, or to a trying interview with some disagreeable individual full of peevishness and quarrelsomeness, you become negative to them. You are then the sponge, drinking in the injurious thought element of the crowded store, the sickly thought element from the sick-bed or hospital, the actual poisonous and subtle element from any person or persons, whose minds put out a quality of thought less healthy or cruder than your own.

If you go fatigued in mind or body among a crowd of wearied, feverish, excited people, your strength is not drawn from you by them, for you have little strength to give. But you absorb, and, for the time being, make their hurried, wearied thought a part of yourself. You have then cast on you a load of lead, figuratively speaking. As you absorb their quality of thought, you will in many things think as they do and see also as they do. You will become discouraged, though before you were hopeful. Your plans for business, which, when by yourself, seemed likely to succeed, will now seem impossible and visionary. You will fear where before you had courage. You will possibly become undecided, and in the recklessness of indecision buy what you do not really need, or do something, or say something, or take some hasty step in business which you would not have done had you been by yourself, thinking your own thoughts, and not the clouded thoughts of the crowd around you. You will possibly return home fagged out and sick in mind and body.

Through these causes, the person whom you may meet an hour hence, or the condition of mind in which you are on meeting that person, may cause success or failure in your most important undertakings. From such a person you may absorb a thought which may cause you to alter your plans, either for success or failure.

If you must mingle among crowds, or with minds whose thoughts are inferior to your own, do so only when you are strongest in mind and body, and leave as soon as you feel wearied. When strong, you are the positive magnet, driving off their injurious thought-element. When weak, you become the negative magnet, attracting their thought to you; and such thought is freighted with physical and mental disease. Positive men are drivers and pushers, and succeed best in the world. Yet it is not well to be always in the positive or force-sending state of mind; if you are, you will divert from you many valuable ideas. There must be a time for the mental reservoir of force or thought to fill up as well as give forth. The person who is always in the positive attitude of mind—he or she who will never hear new ideas without immediately fighting them—who never takes time to give quiet hearing to ideas which may seem wild and extravagant, who insists ever that what does not seem reasonable to him must necessarily be unreasonable for every one else, such a mind will certainly, by constantly maintaining this mental attitude, be drained of all force.

On the other hand, the persons who are always negative or always in the receiving state, those who "never know their own minds" for two hours at a time, who are swayed unconsciously by everyone with whom they talk, who allow themselves, when they go with a plan or a purpose, to be discouraged by a sneer, by a single word of opposition, are as the reservoir, ever filling up with mud and trash, which at last stops the pipe for distributing water; in other words, they have their force-sending capacity almost destroyed, and are unsuccessful in everything which they undertake.

As a rule, you must be positive when you have dealings with the world, for very much the same reason that the pugilist must be positive when he stands before his antagonist. You must be negative when you retire from the ring—from active participation in business. You will tire yourself out by constantly confronting opponents, even in thought, in any sort of contest.

Why did the Christ of Judea so often withdraw from the multitude? It was because, after exercising in some way his Immense power of concentrated thought, either by healing or talking, or by giving some proofs of his command over the physical elements, at which times he was positive and expended his force, he, feeling the negative state coming upon him, left the crowd, so that he should not absorb their lower thought. Had he done so, his force would have been dissipated by carrying such thought, that is, by getting in sympathy with it, feeling it and thinking it, just as you may have done when a person, full of troubles, comes to you, and spends an hour telling those troubles to you, literally pouring into you his load of anxious thought. You sympathize, you are sorry, you desire strongly to help, and, when he leaves, your thought follows him. In such case, your own force is used up by the feeling of sympathy or sorrow, while it might otherwise have been applied to something far more beneficial and profitable in result both to yourself and him.

An orator would not spend an hour previous to his speech in public in carrying bushels of coal upstairs to relieve a tired laborer, for if he did, his strength, brilliancy, inspiration, the force required for his effort, would be mostly used up in the drudgery of carrying coal. The ideas which he puts forth may prove the direct or indirect means of relieving that laborer in some way, and even thousands of others.

You must be positive and restrain the outflow of your sympathetic force very often in the cases of private individuals in trouble, in order to have power to do all the more for them. In politics and professions, the men who live longest and who exercise most influence are those who are least accessible to the masses; for if they are constantly mingling with all manner of people, and so absorbing varied atmospheres, much of their power is wasted in carrying it. Look at the long list of prominent American politicians who have died in the prime of life, or but little past it, during the last few decades; Seward, Grant, Morton, M'Clellan, Logan, Wilson, Hendricks, Chase, Stanton. Not keeping themselves positive—ignorant exposure to all manner of inferior thought atmospheres when negative—has been a most important factor in these premature deaths.

Great financiers like Jay Gould avoid the crowd and hubbub of the Stock Exchange. They live relatively secluded lives, are not easy of access, and transact much business through agents. In so doing, they avoid hurried and confused thought atmospheres. They surround and keep themselves as in a fortress, in the clearer thought-element of the world of finance, and from it derive their keensightedness on their plane of action. They realize the necessity of so doing without possibly being able to define the law. Many methods are quite unconsciously adopted by people which bring successful results in many fields of effort, and which are adopted through the unconscious action and teaching of the laws governing thought.

If you are now very much in the company of some person whose quality of thought is inferior to your own, you are certainly affected injuriously, through absorbing that person's thought since you cannot be positive all the time, to resist the entrance of his thought. When wearied, you are negative, or in a state for receiving his or her thought, and then it must act on you. As so it acts on you, unconsciously you may do many things, in conformity with his or her order of thought, which you would have done differently, and possibly better, had you not been exposed to it and absorbed it.

If so you absorb the element of fear or indecision from anyone, will you act in business with your own natural confidence, courage, energy and determination? It matters not what is the relation to you of those whose temporary or permanent association may thus do you harm, whether that of parent, brother, sister, wife or friend; if their mental growth is less than yours, and if therefore they cannot see as you see, you are very likely to be injured in mind, pocket and health through their constant association. For such reason, Paul the apostle advised people not to be "unequally yoked together in marriage." Why? Because he knew that of any two persons living constantly together, yet occupying different worlds of thought, one would surely be injured; and the one most injured is the highest, finest and broadest mind, which is loaded down, crippled and fettered by the grosser thought absorbed from the inferior.

If you are in active business sympathy or relation with any person who is nervous, excited, irritable, destitute of any capacity for repose, always worried about something, and on the rush from morning till night, though you are separated by hundreds of miles, you will, when in the receiving state, have that person's mind acting injuriously on yours, and you will have thereby sent to you much of his or her cruder thought-element, which, agitating and disturbing your mind, will, in time, work unpleasant results to the body.

Your only means of avoiding this is to cease such relation and common sympathy and effort with them as soon as possible,—to put them out of your mind,—to fix and interest yourself in some other diversion or occupation whenever your thought goes out to them. For every time that you so think, you send out your actual life and vitality in their direction, and thus doing you may transmit a current of life and force which will give them relative success in many undertakings, a success that you may lack, for you are transferring your capital stock of force, while you should use it for yourself. The cruder minds can only appropriate a part of this. The rest is wasted. They may be kept alive by it and prosper, and in return send you only element which brings on you disease, lack of energy and barrenness of idea.

Proper association is one of the greatest of agencies for realizing success, health and happiness. Association here means something far beyond the physical proximity of bodies. You are literally nearest the person or persons of whom you think most, though they are ten thousand miles distant.

If you have been long in association with a person, so absorbing thought-element inferior to your own, you cannot, if you sever the connection, immediately free yourself from the inferior thought-current flowing from him to you, though thousands of miles may intervene. Distance amounts to little in the unseen world of thought. If such a person is much in your thought, his mind still acts on yours, sending you grosser and injurious element. You must learn to forget him if you wish to escape injury. That must be a gradual process. In so forgetting you cut the invisible wires binding you together, through which there have been sent elements injurious to you.

Does this sound cold, cruel and hard? But where is the benefit of two persons being so tied together in thought or remembrance, if one or both are injured? If one is injured so also must be the other in time. But the superior mind receives more immediate injury, and many a person fails to attain the position where he or she should stand, through this cause.

Through this cause also there come disease, lack of vigor, corpulence and clumsiness. The cruder element so sent you by another, and absorbed by you, can materialize itself in physical substance, and make itself seen and felt on your body in the shape of unhealthy and excessive fat, swollen limbs, or any other outward sign of disease and decay. In such case, it is not really your own unwieldy or deformed body that you are carrying about. It is the inferior body of another person sent you in thought; as year after year this process goes on, the cumbrous frame which you so carry becomes at last too heavy for your spirit, and then it drops off. You are "dead," in the estimation of your acquaintances, but you are not really dead; you have simply tumbled down under a load which you could no longer bear.

Even a book in which you are greatly interested, which draws strongly on your sympathy, and has much to say on the mental or physical distress of the person so drawing on your sympathy, can, if you read it in the negative or receiving state, bring to you some form of the physical or mental ailments alluded to therein. Such a book is the representative of the mind of the individual whose history it contains, acting on yours, and bringing to you in thought-element all that person's morbid and unhealthy states of mind, which for a time settle on you and become a parasitical part of you. In this way great harm may be done to sensitive people through reading novels and even true stories full of physical or mental suffering.

If a character to which you are strongly attracted is described as being confined for years in a dungeon, suffering physical and mental pain from such confinement, and in the pages of that book if you follow such life and become absorbed in it, you do actually live therein. You will, if so reading such history day after day, and getting thoroughly absorbed or merged in it, find your vitality or your digestion affected in some way. The law operates, though you may never dream that the cold which you have taken more easily, through lack of vitality, the headache or weakness of digestion, is owing to a mental condition brought on you temporarily through living in the thought of that book while in the receiving state of mind. These are unhealthy books; and so are plays which work strongly on people's emotions in the dramatic representation of scenes of horror, distress and death. The health of thousands on thousands is injured through attracting and fastening on themselves, while in the negative or receiving condition, these unhealthy currents of thought and their consequent unhealthy mental states.

While eating, one should always be in the receptive condition, for then you are gathering material element to nourish the body; and if you eat in a calm, composed, cheerful frame of mind, you are receiving a similar character of thought. To eat and growl, to argue violently or intensely with others, to eat and still think business and plan business, is to be positive, when of all times you should then be negative. It is like working with your body while you eat. You send, while so arguing or grumbling, that force from you which is needed for digestion. It matters little whether you grumble or argue in speech or in thought.

There is also injurious result to you when any person at the table is for any reason—any offensive habit, any peculiarity of manner or mood-unpleasant to you, and you are thereby obliged to endure instead of enjoying his company, for all endurance means the putting out of positive thought— in other words, working in mind to drive off the annoyance. Especially the dinner in the latter part of the day should be the day's climax of happiness—a union of minds in perfect accord with each other—the conversation light, bright, lively and humorous—the palates appreciative of artistic cookery, and the eye also regaled with the appointments of the table and the dining-room. In such a condition and in such receptive state you absorb a spiritual strength, coming from the thought of all about you as they will absorb yours. But if you eat in a social dungeon, in the barrack of a restaurant, where only material food is given, in an unhappy family, full of petty jealousies and complainings, in a boarding-house manger, you may exhaust yourself in resisting or enduring annoyances, thereby lessening the power of digestion and assimilation of your food; and you absorb also more or less of the discontent or moodiness of those about you, and so carry away a load worse than useless—a load which is the real cause of an imperfect digestion, of consequent physical weakness and mental unrest, or irritability.

When you are much alone, you attract and are surrounded by a quality and current of thought coming from minds similar to your own. It is for this reason, that in moments of solitude your thought may be more clear and agreeable than when in the company of others. You live then in another and finer world of ideas. You may deem these ideas but as " idle thoughts "; you may not dare to mention them before others; you may long for company, and may take such as you can get, or you may have it forced upon you. With it your ideal world is shattered, and seems possibly absolute nonsense. You enter into your neighbors' current of thought, their line of talk and motive. You chatter and run on as they do; you criticize, censure, judge and possibly abuse others not present; when you are again by yourself, you feel a sense of discontent with yourself, and a certain vague self-condemnation for what you have been saying. That is your higher mind, your real self, protesting against the injury done it by the lower mind—or not possibly so much your lower mind as the lower thought which you absorb while in that company, and which for a time becomes a parasitical part of you, as the ivy-vine may fasten itself to the oak, from the root to the topmost branch, drawing its nourishment in part from the oak, giving it poison in return, and at last so covering it up that the tree is concealed and is eventually killed thereby.

In a similar manner are refined minds often buried, concealed and prevented their true expression by the lower and parasitical thought, which, unconscious of the evil it can do them, they enter among, associate with and allow to fasten upon them. They are not themselves, and perhaps from their earliest physical life never have been themselves, so far as outward expression goes. They are as oaks buried and concealed by the poisonous ivy. But you may say: "I cannot live alone and without association." True. It is not desirable or profitable that you should. It is not good for man or woman to live alone. It is most desirable, profitable and necessary that you should be fed by the strong, healthy, vigorous, cheerful thought-element coming from minds whose aspiration, ideal and motives are like your own.

When you cut off association or the flow even of your thought from those who are injurious to you, you prevent not only the intrusion of their evil quality of thought but you open the door for the better. You will then by degrees attract, in physical form, those who can give you at once more entertainment and more help. Your highest thought is an unseen force or link, ever connecting you with higher minds akin to your own. These cannot act on you to any extent so long as you continue association or are linked in thought with the lower. Such link or association bars the door to the higher.

How much real comfort, strength, cheer or entertainment do you get from your daily associates? Are they live company? Who does the entertaining, you or they?, who must ever keep up the conversation when it flags? Are you never bored by their prosiness, by all which you have heard over and over again, and if, when on hearing and rehearsing it you do not express discontent in your speech, do you not in your secret thought? How much of the association that you seek, or that seeks you, is really more endured than enjoyed, and is, in fact, only " taken up with " because of the lack of better.

You will never tire of your true and most profitable associates, who, having opened themselves to the higher, are ever drawing in new idea, and with this a new life, which they will give to you, as you give them in return. These are the "wells of water springing up unto everlasting life." These are the "savours of life unto life, and not of death unto death," as are minds to each other who, month after month and year after year, only think in a rut, talk in a rut and act in a rut. These are the dead who should be left to " bury their dead." True life is a state of continuous variety; it involves, through opening the mind in the right direction, and keeping it so open, an endless association with other and like minds, giving ever to each other, and receiving unfailing supply of strength, vigor and the elements of eternal youth.

The fountain of youth, and endless youth, is a spiritual reality, as are many other things which are deemed idle vagaries, and have been erroneously sought on the physical stratum of life. The fountain of endless youth, youth of body as well as mind, lies in the attainment of that mental attitude or condition which is instantly positive to all evil, cruder and lower thought, but negative or receptive to higher and constructive thought, full of courage, devoid of all fear, deeming nothing impossible, hating no individual, disliking only error, full of love for all. but expanding its sympathy wisely and carefully.

Some Practical Mental Recipes

None of us can expect to believe and live up to new laws, principles, or methods of life all at once. Though convinced of their truth, there is an unyielding, stubborn part of us which is hostile to them. That part is our material mind or mind of the body.

There is a supreme power and ruling force which pervades and rules the boundless universe.

You are a part of this power.

You as a part have the faculty of bringing to you by constant silent desire, prayer, or demand more and more of the qualities, belongings, and characteristics of this power.

Every thought of yours is a real thing—a force (say this over to yourself twice).

Every thought of yours is literally building for you something for the future of good or ill.

What, then, Is your mind dwelling on now in any matter? The dark or the bright side? Is it toward others ugly or kind? This is precisely the same as asking, " What kind of life and results are you making for yourself in the future? "

If now you are obliged to live in a tenement house or sit at a very inferior table, or live among the coarse and vulgar, do not say to yourself that you must always so live. Live in mind or imagination in the better house. Sit in imagination at better served tables and among superior people. When you cultivate this state of mind your forces are carrying you to the better. Be rich in spirit, in mind, in imagination, and you will in time be rich in material things. It is the mood of mind you are most in, whether that be groveling or aspiring, that is actually making physical conditions of life in advance for you.

The same law applies to the building up of the body. In imagination live in a strong, agile body, though yours is now a weak one.

Do not put any limits to your future possibilities. Do not say: "I must stop here. I must always rank below this or that great man or woman. My body must weaken, decay, and perish, because in the past so many people's bodies have weakened and perished."

Do not say: "My powers and talents are only of the common order and those of an ordinary person. I shall live and die as millions have done before me."

When you think this, as many do unconsciously, you imprison yourself in an untruth. You bring then to yourself the evil and painful results of an untruth. You bar and fetter your aspiration to grow to powers and possibilities beyond the world's present knowledge. You cut from you the higher truth and possibility.

You have latent in you, some power, some capacity, some shade of talent different from that ever before possessed by any human being. No two minds are precisely alike, for the Infinite Force creates infinite variety in its every expression, whether such expression be a sunset or a mind.

Demand at times to be permanently freed from all fear. Every second of such thought does its little to free you forever from the slavery of fear. The Infinite Mind knows no fear, and it is your eternal heritage to grow nearer and nearer to the Infinite Mind.

We absorb the thought of those with whom we are most in sympathy and association. We graft their mind on our own. If their mind is inferior to ours and not on the same plane of thought, we, in such absorption, take in and cultivate an inferior and injurious mental graft.

If you will keep company with people who are reckless and unaspiring, who have no aim or purpose in life, who have no faith in themselves or anything else, you place yourself in the thought current of failure. Your tendency then will be to failure. Because from such people, your closest associates, you will absorb their thought. If you absorb it, you will think it. You will get into the same mood of mind as theirs. If you think as they do, you will in many things find yourself acting as they do, no matter how great your mental gifts.

Your mind surely absorbs the kind of thought it is most with. If you are with the successful you absorb thought which brings success. The unsuccessful are ever sending from them thoughts of lack of order, lack of system, lack of method, or recklessness and discouraged thought. Your mind if much with theirs will certainly absorb these thoughts exactly as a sponge does water.

It is better for your art or business that you have no intimate company at all than the company of reckless, careless, slipshod, and slovenly minds.

When in your mind you cut yourself off from the unlucky and thriftless, your body will not long remain so near theirs. You get then into another force or current. It will carry you into the lives of more successful people.

When you don't know what to do in any matter of business, in anything—wait. Do nothing about it. Dismiss it as much as you can from your mind. Your purpose will be as strong as ever. You are then receiving and accumulating force to put on that purpose. It comes from the Supreme Power. It will come in the shape of an idea, an inspiration, an event, an opportunity. You have not stopped while you so waited. You have all that time been carried to the idea, the inspiration, the event, the opportunity, and it also has been carried or attracted to you.

When in any undertaking we put our main dependence and trust in an individual or individuals and not in the Supreme Power, we are off the main track of the most perfect success.

The highest and real success means, in addition to wealth, increasing health, vigor, and a growth never ceasing into powers and possibilities not yet realized by the race.

As regards your business, don't talk to anybody, man or woman, regarding your plans or projects, or anything connected with them, unless you are perfectly sure they wish for your success. Don't talk to people who hear you out of politeness. Every word so spoken represents so much force taken out of your project. The number you can talk to with profit is very small. But the good wish of one real friend, if he give you a hearing but for ten minutes, is a literal, living, active force, added to your own, and from that time working in your behalf.

If your aim is for right and justice you will be led to those you can trust and talk to with safety. Your spiritual being or sense will tell you whom you can trust.

When you demand justice for yourself, you demand it for the whole race. If you allow yourself to be dominated, brow-beaten, or cheated by others without inward or outward protest, you are condoning deceit and trickery. You are in league with it.

Three persons engaged in any form of gossip, tattle, or scandal generate a force and send it from them of tattle, gossip, and scandal. The thought they send into the air returns to them and does them injury in mind and body. It is far more profitable to talk with others of things which go to work out good. Every sentence you speak is a spiritual force to you and others for good or ill.

Ten minutes spent in growling at your luck, or in growling at others because they have more luck than yourself, means ten minutes of your own force spent in making worse your own health and fortune. Every thought of envy or hatred sent another is a boomerang. It flies back to you and hurts you. The envy or dislike we may feel toward those who, as some express it, " put on airs," the ugly feeling we may have at seeing others riding in carriages and "rolling in wealth,' represents just so much thought (I. e. force) most extravagantly expended, for in its expenditure we get not only unhappiness but destroy future fortune and happiness.

If this has been your common habit or mood of mind, do not expect to get out of it at once. Once you are convinced of the harm done you by such mood, a new force has come to gradually remove the old mind and bring a new one. But all changes must be gradual.

Your own private room is your chief workshop for generating your spiritual force and building yourself up. If it is kept in disorder, if things are flung recklessly about, and you cannot lay your hands instantly upon them, it is an indication that your mind is in the same condition, and therefore your mind as it works on others, in carrying out your projects, will work with less effect and result by reason of its disordered and disorganized condition.

Ill-temper or despondency is a disease. The mind subject to it in any degree a sick mind. The sick mind makes the sick body. The great majority of the sick are not in bed.

When you are peevish, remember your mind is sick. Demand then a well mind.

When you say to yourself, "I am going to have a pleasant visit or a pleasant journey," you are literally sending elements and forces ahead of your body that will arrange things to make your visit or journey pleasant. When before the visit or the journey or the shopping trip you are in a bad humor, or fearful or apprehensive of something unpleasant, you are sending unseen agencies ahead of you which will make some kind of unpleasantness.

Our thoughts, or in other words, our state of mind, is ever at work " fixing up " things good or bad for us in advance.

As you cultivate this state of mind more and more you will at last have no need of reminding yourself to get into such mood. Because the mood will have become a part of your everyday nature, and you cannot then get out of it, or prevent the pleasant experiences it will bring you.

Our real self is that which we cannot see, hear, or feel with the physical senses—our mind. The body is an instrument it uses. We are then made up entirely of forces we call thoughts. When these thoughts are evil or immature they bring us pain and ill-fortune. We can always change them for better thoughts or forces. Earnest steady desire for a new mind (or self) will surely bring the new mind and more successful self. And this will ever be changing through such desire for the newer and ever more successful self.

All of us do really "pray without ceasing." We do not mean by prayer any set formality or form of words. A person who sets his or her mind on the dark side of life, who lives over and over the misfortunes and disappointments of the past, prays for similar misfortunes and disappointments in the future. If you will see nothing but ill luck in the future, you are praying for such ill luck and will surely get it.

You carry into company not only your body, but what is of far more importance, your thought or mood of mind, and this thought or mood, though you say little or nothing, will create with others an impression for or against you, and as it acts on other minds will bring you results favorable or unfavorable according to its character.

What you think is of far more importance than what you say or do. Because your thought never for a moment ceases its action on others or whatever it is placed upon. Whatever you do has been done because of a previous, long held mood or state of mind before such doing.

The thought or mood of mind most profitable in permanent results to you is the desire to do right. This is not sentiment, but science. Because the character of your thought brings to you events, persons, and opportunities with as much certainty as the state of the atmosphere brings rain or dry weather.

To do right is to bring to yourself the best and most lasting result for happiness. You must prove this for yourself.

Doing right is not, however, doing what others may say or think to be right. If you have no standard of right and wrong of your own, you are acting always on the standard held or made by others.

Your mind is always working and acting on other minds to your advantage or disadvantage whether your body is asleep or awake. Your real being in the form of a thought travels like electricity through space. So when you lay the body down to sleep, see that your mind is in the best mood to get during your physical unconsciousness the best things. For if you go to sleep angry or despondent your thought goes straight to the unprofitable domain of anger or despondency, and will bring to your physical life on awakening, first the element and afterwards that ill success which anger and despondency always attract.

Health is involved in the Biblical adage, " Let not the sun go down on your wrath." Every mood of mind you get into brings to you flesh, bone, and blood of a quality or character like itself. People who from year to year live in moods of gloom or discouragement are building elements of gloom and discouragement into their bodies, and the ill results cannot be quickly removed.

The habit of hurry wears out more bodies and kills more people than is realized. If you put on your shoes hurriedly while dressing in the morning you will be very apt to be in a hurry all day. Pray to get out of the current of hurried thought into that of repose. Hurried methods of doing business lose many thousands of dollars. Power to keep your body strong and vigorous—power to have influence with people worth holding—power to succeed in your undertakings comes of that reposeful frame of mind which while doing relatively little with the body, sees far ahead and clearly in mind.

So, when in the morning, be you man or woman, you look at what is to be done and begin to feel yourself overwhelmed and hurried by the household cares, the writing, the shopping, the people to be seen, the many things to be done, sit right down for thirty seconds and say, " I will not be mobbed and driven in mind by these duties. I will now proceed to do one thing—one thing alone, and let the rest take care of themselves until it is done." The chances are then that the one thing will be done well. If that is done well, so will all the rest. And the current of thought you bring to you in so cultivating this mood will bear you to far more profitable surroundings, scenes, events, and associations than will the semi-insane mood and current of hurry.

All of us believe in many untruths today. It is an unconscious belief. The error is not brought before our minds. Still we go on acting and living in accordance with our unconscious error, and the suffering we may experience comes from that wrong belief.

Demand, then, every day ability to see our wrong beliefs. We need not be discouraged if we see many more than we think we have at present. They cannot be seen and remedied all at once.

Don't take a " tired feeling " or one of languor in the day time for a symptom of sickness. It is only your mind asking for rest from some old rut of occupation.

If your stomach is disordered make your mind responsible for it. Say to yourself, " This disagreeable feeling comes of an error in thought." If you are weak or nervous, don't lay the fault on your body. Say again, "It is a state of my mind which causes this physical ailment, and I demand to get rid of such state and get a better one." If you think any medicine or medical advice will do you good, by all means take it, but mind and keep this thought behind it: " I am taking this medicine not to help my body but as an aid to my spirit,"

Your child is a mind which having lost the body it used in a past physical existence (and possibly of another race and country), has received a new one, as you did in your own infancy.

Tell your child never to think meanly of itself. For if it becomes habituated to such thought, others will feel it and think of the child first and of the grown-up person afterwards as of small value.

Nothing damages the individual more than self-deprecation, and many a child Is weighted down with the elements of failure before it goes into the world through years of scolding, snubbing, and telling it that it is a worthless being.

Tell your child in all its plans to see or think only success. To keep in the permanent mood of expecting success, brings causes, events, and opportunities, which bring success.

Let us also tell this to ourselves very often, for we are but children also, with physical bodies a few years older than the infants.

We have as yet but the vaguest idea of what life really means, and the possibilities it has in store for us. One attribute of the relatively perfected life to come to this race is the retention or preservation of a physical body so long as the mind or spirit desires it. It will be a body also free from pain and sickness, and one which can be made or unmade, put on or taken off, at will.

Say of anything that "it must be done" and you are putting out a mighty unseen power for doing. When your mind is in the mood of ever saying "must," whether you have in mind the particular thing you aim at or not, still that force is ever working on your purpose. But we need to be careful as to what that force of "must" is put on. "Must" without asking for wisdom as to where it shall be placed may bring you terrible results.

Always in your individual aims and purposes defer to the Higher Power and Infinite Wisdom. The thing you may most desire might prove a curse.

Be always, then, in the mood of saying, "There is a Power which knows what will bring me the most permanent happiness better than I do. If my desire is not good let it not come, for in its place I shall have something better."

If you send your thought in sympathy to everyone who calls for it, you may have very little left to help yourself. It is necessary to have great care in the choice of those on whom we put our love and thought. One may help build us up; another tear us down. We need to ask for wisdom that we may know whom to receive in close association.

As you are a part of God or the Supreme Power, and a peculiar part, you can always estimate yourself as the very best of such peculiar part. No one else can approach or equal or excel you, as you represent and put out your own peculiar powers, gifts, or shades of mind and character. You will in time command the world of your own mind, and while others may compel your admiration, you will do yourself a great injury if you worship them or abase yourself or grovel before them even in mind.

Idolatry is the blind worship of anything or any body save the Infinite Force from which alone you draw life, power, and inspiration.

The thought of a woman coming to you, or a man, in sympathy or love, with ideas, aims, and aspirations equal to or above yours, may prove to you a source of strength of muscle, health of body, and clearness of mind. His or her thought so flowing to you is a real element. If a man or woman inferior to you mentally is your companion or much in your thought, your mind will be much less clear and your health will eventually suffer.

Be you man or woman, your life cannot be complete and you cannot build yourself rapidly into higher and higher powers until you meet and recognize spiritually your eternal complement or completement in the other sex. And from such complement there is no departure.

When we eat and drink let us remember that with every mouthful we place and build a thought into our selves in accordance with the mood we are in while eating. So be sure to be bright, hopeful, and buoyant while eating, and if you cannot command such mood of mind, pray for it. To ask night and morning of the Supreme Power for the highest wisdom (that is, the greatest good and happiness), and to demand this in that frame of mind which acknowledges the superiority of that Wisdom over your own, is certainly to put yourself in the current of the greatest and most enduring health and prosperity. Because another and better current of thought then begins to act on you and will gradually carry you out of errors and into the right. It will lead you by degrees into different surroundings, different ways of living, and will in time bring you the association you really need and what is best for you.

Self-teaching; Or, the Art of Learning How to Learn

It is a commonly received opinion, that in youth it is easier to learn than in after years; that at "middle age," or after, the mind becomes, as it were, set in a rut or mold, which does not readily receive new impressions. This idea is expressed in the adage: "You can't teach an old dog new tricks."

People have made this a truth by accepting it as a truth. It is not a truth. If your mind is allowed to grow and strengthen, it will learn more easily and quickly than during the infancy of the body. It will learn more and more quickly how, to learn any new thing. Learning how to learn, learning how to grasp at the principles underlying any art, is a study and a science by itself.

The child, in most cases, does not learn so quickly as many suppose. Think of the years often spent at school, from the age of six to sixteen or eighteen, and how little, relatively, is learned during that period. But this time of life is not regarded as of so much importance as that after eighteen or twenty. He or she would be deemed to have a dull intellect, who should require fourteen years to gain only so much as what a large proportion of children gain from the age of six to twenty.

It is possible for any man or woman whose mind has grown to that degree, that they can acknowledge that every possibility exists within themselves to learn any art, any profession, any business, and become skilled therein, and this even without teachers, and at the period termed "middle age," or after, providing,

First, That they are in living earnest to learn.

Second, That they fight obstinately against the idea of " can't," or that they are too old to learn.

Third. That in all effort to become proficient in their new calling, they cease such effort as soon as it becomes fatiguing or irksome, and that they make of such effort a recreation, and not a drudgery.

Fourth, That they allow no other person to argue, sneer, or ridicule them out of the truth that the human mind can accomplish anything it sets its forces persistently upon.

Fifth, That they keep their minds in the attitude of ever desiring, demanding, praying for whatever quality or trait of character or temperament they need to succeed in their effort; and that whenever the thought of such effort is in mind, it shall be accompanied with this unspoken thought: "I will do what I have set out to do."

There should be no "hard study" at any age. Real "study" is easy and pleasing mental effort; as when you watch the motion of an animal that awakens your curiosity, of a person that interests you. You are studying when you admire and examine the structure of a beautiful flower; you are studying the method and style of an actor or actress when they most hold and compel your attention and admiration. All admiration is in reality study. When you admire anything that is beautiful, your mind is concentrated upon it. You are quite unconsciously examining it. You remember, without effort, many of its features, or characteristics. That unforced examination and attention is study.

To "study hard " is to try to admire; to try to admire is to try to love; to try to love, or to be forced by others to try to love, generally ends in hating the thing or pursuit so forced upon you,—one reason why so often the schoolboy hates "to learn his lesson."

The experience of those who have gone before us in any art, trade, occupation, or profession, is unquestionably valuable, but valuable only as suggestion. There is a great deal laid down as rules and "canons of art" which shackle and repress originality. The idea is constantly, though indirectly, impressed on learners, that the utmost limit of perfection has been reached in some art by some " old master," and that it would be ridiculous to think of surpassing him.

Now, genius knows no "old master." It knows no set form of rules made for it by others. It makes its own rules as it goes along, as did Shakespeare, Byron, and Scott in literature, and the first Napoleon in war; and your mind may have in it the seed of some new idea, discovery, invention, some new rendering of art in some form, which the world never saw before.

Any man or woman who loves to look at trees and flowers, lakes and rivulets, waves, waterfalls, and clouds, has within him or her the faculty for imitating them in the effects of light, shade, and color,—has, in brief, a taste for painting.

You say, "People to be artists, must have the art born within them." I say, " If they admire the art, they have within them the faculty for advance in that art."

You say, " But because I admire a rose, or a landscape, it is no sign I can ever paint either." I say, "Yes, you can, providing you really want to.

But how! Put your effort on it for an hour, half an-hour, fifteen minutes, a day. Begin. Begin anywhere. Anything in this world will do for a starting point. Begin, and try to imitate on paper a dead leaf, a live one, a stone, a rock, a log, a box, a brickbat. A brickbat lying in the mud has lying with it light, shade and color, and the laws governing them, as much as a cathedral, and is a better foundation than a cathedral to begin on. Begin with the stub of a pencil, on the back of an old envelope. Every minute of such work after beginning is so much practice gained. Every minute before such beginning, providing you intend to begin, and do not, is so much practice lost, as regards that particular art.

Mind, however, you make of such practice a recreation, just as boys do in ball throwing and catching, or as the billiard player does who takes up the cue for half-an-hour, matched only against himself, or as the horseman does who exercises the horse for practice before the race. When the work becomes irksome, when you get out of patience, because your brickbat won't come out on the paper like the original, drop it, wait for your patience-reservoir to fill up, and take for your next copy a log, a tree trunk, or anything else.

You say that you should go to a teacher of this or that art, so that you can become " properly grounded in its principles," and that, by such teacher's aid, you shall avoid blundering and stumbling along, making little or no progress.

Take up any trade, any handicraft, any art, all by yourself, and grope along in it by yourself for a few weeks, and at the end of that time you will have many well-defined and intelligent questions to ask about it, of someone more experienced in it than yourself,—the teacher. That is the time to go to the teacher. The teacher should come in when an interest in the art or study is awakened. To have him before, is like answering questions before they are asked.

You cannot teach a dog to paint. The intelligence using the dog's organization has not grown to an appreciation of such imitation of natural objects. But you can teach him to draw a cart, to "point" to game in the cover, to swim out to the water-fowl you have shot, and bring it to you. Why? Because the dog has these instincts, or desires, born in him. The trainer, his teacher, brings them out. Some men and women have no more admiration for a beautiful landscape than the dog. Of course, neither can ever be taught to paint, because they have not the desire to paint, nor the admiration of the thing to be painted.

"Then, whatever a man or woman really desires to do, is to be taken as some proof that they can do it? " you ask. "Yes; that is the exact idea." Desire to accomplish is a proof of ability to accomplish. Of course, such ability may be weighted down and kept back by many causes, such as ill-health of body, ill-health of mind, unfavorable surroundings, and, perhaps, greatest of all, utter ignorance that such desire is a proof of the possession of power to accomplish the thing desired.

How did you learn to walk, and how did you learn to talk? Could anyone have taught you, if desire to walk and talk had not been born with you? Did you go to a walking teacher, or a talking teacher? Did you not learn both accomplishments after ten thousand failures? So far as you can remember, was it not rather an amusement than otherwise, to learn both, or at least, was there any idea of work associated with these early efforts?

You place a boy or girl by the water-side, and give them full liberty, and they will learn to swim as naturally as they learn to walk, because the desire to swim is in them. If, after learning, they see a better swimmer, they will naturally try to imitate him; and all this endeavor, from first to last, will be for them far more recreation than work. The better swimmer who comes along represents the teacher; and the boy and girl who can already swim fairly well, and are anxious to swim better, represent pupils who are in a condition to be taught.

Think for a moment, how much it was necessary to teach your body in training it to walk. First, to balance yourself upright on two feet without falling. Secondly, to balance yourself on one foot without falling. Thirdly, to move the body. Fourthly, to give it the direction in which you wanted to go. And yet we call walking a "mechanical," and not a mental, effort.

If you are determined to paint, and love the creations of nature and art well enough to try and imitate them, you will be constantly studying effects in light and shade on rocks, stones, cliffs, towers, steeples. You will observe and study, and be rejoiced at the many changing aspects and colors of the sky, as you never were before. You will discover, as you continue to observe, that nature has a different shade of color for every day of the year, and almost every hour of the day. You will suddenly find in all this a new and permanent recreation, without money and without price. You will then find new interests and new sources of amusement in studying the works of painters and their methods, which will be revealed to you just so fast as your appreciation grows up to them.

The same principle will apply to any branch of mechanics or art,—to anything. Of course, it is best to pursue that for which you have the most inclination, that is, admiration. If you are in any occupation that does not suit you, and you want to engage in some art that does suit you, if you have fifteen minutes in the day to spare, begin on that art.

If it is painting, paint a brickbat in some idle moment as well as you can, and only as a means of amusement. If it is carving, you have always the means for practice, if you have a jack-knife and a bit of wood. If it be music, a banjo or guitar with but a single string will give you means for practice. For you must commence in the simplest way, even as you crept before you walked. There must be imperfect effort before there can be relatively perfect result.

Because, when you do so begin, you begin to practice with one instrument far more ingenious and complicated than any you can buy for use in your art; namely, your mind.

If we begin in this way, we begin something else; we begin drawing toward us ways, means, helps, and agencies unseen, but powerful, to help us. We are not to expect success in an hour, a day, a month, a year. But if we persist, a relative success is coming all the while. The effort of this month is better than that of last. There may come periods of weariness and discouragement; periods when, as we look back, we seem to have made no advance; periods, in fact, when we seem to have gone back, when we seem to be doing worse than at the start; periods when we lose all interest in the work. It makes us sick to look at it, even to think of taking it up again; and a certain sense of guilt at our neglect intensifies the sickness.

That is a mistake. If, in our music, our painting, our profession, our business, be it what it may, we strive for some certain result, and fail, time after time, and week after week, to effect it, yet we are still advancing towards it.

We may not see such advance. That is because the advance is not in the direction we think it should be. There may be a screw loose in a part of our mental being that we have taken no note of, which keeps us back. That screw, in very many cases, lies in the state of mind in which we take up our work or pursuit.

We may be too anxious or impatient. We take up the pen, the brush, or the tool, in a hurried frame of mind. We want to do too many things at once. Or we endeavor to crowd the doing of several things in too short a limit of time. Or we are unable to dismiss all thought, save what bears on the effort now in hand.

All such moods are destructive to the best effort. They take much of our force from that effort. A common result is that we can do nothing to suit us. We throw down our work in disgust. We may not take it up again for weeks. We do take it up at last, perhaps, in a listless, indifferent frame of mind. We do not then set our hearts on doing anything perfect, or making it come up to our ideal in a moment, and that Is the very time when we produce some new effect; when we hit the idea we have aimed at; when we are surprised at the apparently accidental development of a new power within us.

There is a great mystery in this,—a mystery we may never solve,—the mystery that whatever purpose this power within us we call mind sets itself upon, fixes itself upon persistently, that purpose it is accomplishing, that purpose it is carrying out, that purpose it is ever drawing nearer to itself, not only when we work for it with the body and the intellect; we are also growing ever towards it when it seems for the time forgotten, or when we are asleep.

That persistent purpose, that strong desire, that never-ceasing longing, is a seed in the mind. It is rooted there. It is alive. It never stops growing. Why this is so, we may never know. Perhaps it is not desirable to know. It is enough to know that it is so. There is a wonderful law involved in it. This law, when known, followed out, and trusted, leads every individual to mighty and beautiful results. This law, followed with our eyes open, leads to more and more happiness in life; but followed blindly, involuntarily with our eyes shut, leads to misery.

To succeed in any undertaking, any art, any trade, any profession, simply keep it ever persistently fixed in mind as an aim, and then study to treat all effort towards it as play, recreation. The moment it becomes "hard work," we are not advancing. I mean by "play," that both body and mind work easily and pleasantly. It matters not what a man or woman is doing, whether digging sand or scrubbing floors, when the mind is interested in that work and the muscles are full of strength, such work is play, and is more apt to be well done. When the muscles are exhausted of their power, and will alone drives the body forward, the occupation soon becomes work, drudgery, and is much the more apt to be ill done. I begin low down in illustration, as low as sand, mud, brickbats; but the principle is the same, be the worker a hod-carrier or a Michael Angelo.

The science of learning to learn, then, involves largely that of making recreation of all effort. This is not as easy as it may seem. It involves a continual prayer for patience, patience, patience.

"Patience to play?" you ask. Yes. When we are amused by any effort of our own, be it effort of the eye, in seeing sights that please it, or effort of the ear, in hearing sounds that please it, or effort of muscle in exercising them, that is the very time when we are most attentive and most absorbed. The very time when we forget there is such a thing as patience, is the very time we most exercise patience.

That is the mood we need to cultivate. Because moods of mind determine the character and quality of effort. The painter writes out his mood in his picture; a mistake, a blur, a defect, a daub, may write out in that picture too much hurry to get ahead. He took up his brush, possibly, full of irritation, because his wife asked him for more money for household expenses; result, he puts a woman in that picture twelve feet high as proportioned to other objects, when she should have been but four. What put on that extra and needless eight feet? A mood born of household expenses. Or the scrubber wrote out her mood of mind on the floor. Where? In that neglected corner, where the last dust of summer lingers alone. Why? Because her mood of hurry to be through with her work is there written; or her mood of dishonesty, in doing as little as possible for the money to be received; or her mood of anxiety concerning the sick child, left at home in some squalid tenement; or the poor woman's mood born of physical weakness, in thus trying to do a man's work, with no nutritious food in her stomach, and no money to buy any till the work is done.

My very practical friend, you who despise all "art flummery," all and everything that is not "business," and smells of wood, or stone, or leather, or bank-bills, this cultivation of the mood is of vast importance to you, also; because, when you meet your brother Hard Cash, to have a wrangle over bargain and sale, the man who is in the coolest mood, the most collected mood, the mood most free of other thought, or care, the man who is in the least hurry, the man who throws overboard all anxiety as to results, the man who is not too eager, who can lie back in his chair and make a joke or laugh at you, when millions are trembling in the balance, who keeps all his reserve force till it is needed, that is the man who can play the best hand in your game, and make the best bargain. That is the man who gains his end by some knowledge of spiritual law; and spiritual law can be used for all purposes, and purposes relatively low as well as high; and in some things the wicked, so-called, of today, are better informed in certain phases of spiritual law than those who call themselves good.

How shall we get ourselves, then, into the most desirable mood for doing our best? By praying for it, asking for it, demanding it, in season and out of season. We can wish an earnest desire in a second, no matter where we are. That is a prayer. It is a thought that goes out, and does its work in bringing us another atom of the quality desired. That atom is never lost. It adds itself to and adds its strength to all the other atoms of the same quality so gained. So you call this simple? Is the method too easy? Remember, we are indeed fearfully and wonderfully made; and when Solomon wrote this he had an inkling of the existence of powers wrapped up in human bodies, that startled him, and would us, did we more fully realize them.

Possibly this question may be asked: "What is the use of cultivating, or encouraging others to cultivate any form of art, when for thousands the struggle is so hard today for bread?" Or, in other words, " What is the use of educating people to wants and desires they cannot satisfy?" Or, " What bearing and benefit has art cultivation in righting the 'great wrongs' of the hour?"

It is of the greatest possible benefit. Art, art appreciation, art cultivation, refines human nature. Refinement demands finer surroundings, finer food, finer houses, cleaner houses, cleaner clothes, cleaner skin. You can't make people clean, neat, tasteful, by telling them they "ought" to be so. They must have brought out of them some calling, some occupation, some work which will implant ever-increasing desire for more of the allegiances of life. Much of what is called the

"oppression" of the strong over the weak, the rich over the poor, comes because so many of the poor do not aspire above a pig-pen under the window, a mud-puddle in the back-yard, and a front garden growing tomato cans, dead cats, and old hoop-skirts. Much of the money today given in charity to the poor, is really poured from one rich man's pocket into that of another, and relieves only a temporary distress.

You roll half a ton of coal this winter into the poor man's cellar. His family are warmed for the hour. The profits go into the safe of the coal corporation. Its heat warms human beings with little ambition above animals. You encourage that man's boy or girl to paint ever so roughly with the cheapest of water-colors, to mold forms in clay, to have any faculty awakened which shall show them what a beautiful world they really live in, and soon with this there may come a growing distaste for the mud-puddle in the back-yard, and the display of hoopskirts and tomato cans in the front. Show these children that they have within them more or less of this mighty and mysterious element—mind, and that through its exercise they can become almost anything to which they aspire, and that the more of the Infinite Spirit they call to themselves, the more will the have to strengthen, beautify, enrich, invigorate, and electrify their souls and bodies, and you have then started them on the road of doing for themselves, by the powers in themselves. They are then on a road leading away from both charitable soup-kitchens and gin-shops.

If they cultivate the love of grace and beauty in any direction, they cultivate also an ability for expressing such grace and beauty. If they follow the law of persistent demand for improvement in such grace or beauty, whether it be by the exercise of pen or tongue, of painting or sculpture, or self-command, or polish of manner, or the art of actor, elocutionist. musician, or worker on stone, worker in metal, cultivator of plant, tree, flower, they will at last do something a little better than anyone else can do, in their peculiar way, and through their self-taught, peculiar method; and when they can do this, the world will gladly come to them, and bring them its dollars and cents, for what they can please it with.

None of us know what is in us till we try to bring it out; A man, or woman, may go their whole life with some wonderful power, some remarkable talent which would benefit and please mankind, feeling it ever from time to time, struggling for expression in a desire to use it, in a longing to express it, yet having it ever forced back by that fatal thought, "I can't."

"It's no use." " It's ridiculous, the idea of my aspiring to such a thing." We are treasure boxes, holding wondrous powers. We brought these treasures with us into the world from an immeasurably far-off past—a past we may not compute—a past the spirit, born into being, the tiniest atom, the faintest movement, drawing to itself ever, age after age, through unconscious exercise of desire or demand, more and more of power, more and more of complex organization, more and more of variety of talent, more and more of the marvelous power coming through combination and re-combination of element, until at last the man is born, the woman is born, blind at first, blind as millions now are regarding the wealth within them; blind to faith and belief in themselves, until the veil is pulled from their eyes, and then they shall soon spring up into gods, destined to a career of eternal life, eternal growth, and eternal and illimitable happiness.

Love Thyself

Christ's Precepts say: " Love thy neighbor as thyself." Some people incline to forget the two last words "as thyself," and infer that we should love others even better than ourselves. So far has this idea been carried that it has led in cases to entire sacrifice and neglect of self so that good may be done to others. There is a justifiable and righteous love for self. There can be no true spiritual growth without this higher love for self. Spiritual growth implies the cultivation and increase of every faculty and talent. It means the making of the symmetrically developed man and woman. Spiritual growth, fostered by unceasing demand of the Supreme Power, will bring power to keep the body in perfect health—so as to escape pain and disease—and will eventually carry man above the present limited conditions of mortality. The higher love of self benefits others as well as ourselves.

When we love a person, we send that person our quality of thought. If it is the aspiring order of thought, it is for that person a literal element and agency of life and health in proportion to his or her capacity for absorbing and assimilating it. If we think meanly of ourselves—if we are beggarly in spirit—and are content to live on the bounty of others, if we care little for our personal appearance —if we are willing to get money by questionable means—if we believe there is no Supreme and overruling Power, governing our lives by an exact law, but that everything is left to chance, and that life is only a scramble for existence, we send in thought such beliefs to that person, and if our love is accepted it is only a means to drag down instead of a power to elevate.

How can we send the highest love to another if we do not have it for ourselves? If we are careless and unappreciative of the body's great use to us—if we never give it a thought of admiration or gratitude for the many functions which it performs for us —if we regard it with the same indifference that we may have for the post to which we hitch a horse, we shall send that same quality of sentiment and thought to the person of whom we think most, and the tendency will be to generate a similar disregard for themselves. Either they will do this, or seeking light of the Infinite, they will find themselves obliged in self-protection to refuse the love which we send them, because of its coarser and grosser quality. This is sometimes the error of mothers, who say: " I don't care for myself so that my son or daughter's welfare is assured. I give and devote my whole life to them."

This means: "I am content to grow old and unattractive, I am content to slave and drudge so that my children may receive a good education and shine in society. I am an old and decaying weather-beaten hulk and can't hold together much longer; the best use which I can make of myself is to serve as a sort of foot-bridge for them in the shape of nurse, grandmother and overseer of the nursery and kitchen, while they are playing their parts in society." The daughter receives this thought with the mother's inferior, self-neglecting love. She absorbs and assimilates it. It becomes part of her being. She lives it, acts it out, and thirty years afterwards is saying and doing the same and laying herself upon the shelf with the rest of the cracked teapots for her own daughter's sake.

Ancestral traits of character, as bequeathed and transmitted from parent to child, are the thoughts of the parent absorbed by the child. When in thought, desire and aspiration we make the most of what the Infinite has given us (inclusive of these wonderful bodies), we shall have continual increase, and such increase will overflow of its own accord and benefit others. The highest love for self means justice to self. If we are unjust to ourselves, we shall be unavoidably unjust to those to whom we are of the greatest value. A general who should deprive himself of necessary food and give all his bread and meat to a hungry soldier, might in so doing weaken his body, and with his body weaken his mental faculties, lessen his capacity for command, thereby increasing the chances for the destruction of his entire army.

What is most necessary to know, and what the Infinite will show us if we demand, is the value which we are to others. In proportion to our power for increasing human happiness, and in proportion as we recognize that power, will the needful agencies come to us for making our material condition more comfortable. No man or woman can do their best work for themselves or others who lives in a hovel, dresses meanly and starves the spirit by depriving it of the gratification of its finer tastes. Such persons will always carry the atmosphere and influence of the hovel with them, and that is brutalizing and degrading. If the Infinite worked on such a basis, would the heavens show the splendor of the suns? Would the fields reflect that glory in the myriad hues of leaf and flower, in plumage of bird and hue of rainbow?

What in many cases prevents the exercise of this higher love and justice to self is the thought; "What will others say, and how will others judge me, if I give myself what I owe to myself?" That is, you must not ride in your carriage until every needy relative has a carriage also. The general must not nourish his body properly because the hungry soldier might say that he was rioting in excess. When we appeal to the Supreme and our life is governed by a principle , we are not actuated either fear of public opinion or love of others' approbation, and we may be sure that the Supreme will sustain us. If in any way we try to live to suit others, we shall never suit them; the more we try, the more unreasonable and exacting do they become. The government of your life is a matter which lies entirely between God and yourself; when your life Is swayed and influenced from any other source you are on the wrong path.

Very few people really love themselves. Very few really love their own bodies with the higher love. That higher love puts ever-increasing life in the body and ever-increasing capacity to enjoy life. Some place all their love on the apparel which they place on their bodies; some on the food they put in their bodies; some on the use or pleasure they can get from their bodies. That is not real love for self which gluts the body with food or keeps it continually under the influence of stimulants. It is not a real love for self which indulges to excess in any pleasure to be obtained from the body. The man who racks and strains his body and mind in the headlong pursuit of pleasures or business, loves that business or art unwisely. He has no regard for the instrument on which he is dependent for the materialization of his ideas. This is like the mechanic who should allow a costly tool, by which he is enabled to do rare and elaborate work, to rust or be otherwise injured through neglect. That is not the highest love for self which puts on its best and cleanest apparel when it goes out to visit or promenade and wears ragged or soiled clothes indoors. That is love of the opinion or approbation of others. Such a person only dresses physically. There is a spiritual dressing of the body when the mind in which apparel is put on is felt by others. Whoever has it in any degree will show it in a certain style of carrying his clothes which no tailor can give.

The miser does not love himself. He loves money better than self. To live with a half-starved body, to deny self of every luxury, to get along with the poorest and cheapest things, to deprive self of amusement and recreation in order to lay up money, is surely no love for the whole self. The miser's love is all in his money-bags, and his body soon shows how little love is put in it. Love Is an element as literal as air or water. It has many grades of quality with different people. Like gold, it may be mixed with grosser element. The highest and purest love comes to him or her who is most in communion and oneness with the Infinite Mind, is ever demanding of the Infinite Mind more and more of its wisdom. The regard and thought of such persons is of great value to anyone on whom it is directed. And such persons will, through that wisdom, be wisely economical of their sympathy for others and put a great deal of this higher love into themselves in order to make the most of themselves.

Some people infer from their religious teachings that the body and its functions are inherently vile and depraved; that they are a clog and an encumbrance to any higher and more divine life; that they are corruptible "food for worms," destined to return to dust and molder in the earth. It has been held that the body should be mortified, that the flesh should be crucified and starved and subjected to rigorous penance and pains for its evil tendencies. Even youth, with its freshness, beauty, vigor and vivacity, has been held as almost a sin, or as a condition especially prone to sin. When a person in any way mortifies and crucifies the body, either by starving it, dressing meanly, or living in bare and gloomy surroundings, he generates and literally puts in the body the thought of hatred for itself.

Hatred of others or of self is a slow thought-poison. A hated body can never be symmetrical or healthy. The body is not to be refined and purged of the lower and animal tendencies being made responsible and continually blamed these sins—by being counted as a clod and an encumbrance, which it is fortunate at last to shake off.

Religion, so-called, has in the past made a scapegoat of the body, accused it of every sin, and, in so doing and thinking, has filled it with sin. As one result, the professors of such religion have suffered pain and sickness. Their bodies have decayed, and death has often been preceded by long and painful illness. " By their fruits ye shall know them." The fruits of such a faith and condition of mind prove error therein.

There is a mind of the body—a carnal or material mind—a mind belonging to the instrument used by the spirit. It is a mind or thought lower or crude than that of the spirit. But this mind of the body need not, as has been held, be ever at war with the higher mind of the spirit. It can, through demand of the Infinite, be made in time to act in perfect accord with the spirit. The Supreme Power can and will send us a supreme love for the body. That love we need to have. Not to love one's body is not to love one expression of the Infinite Mind.

We are not inferring that you "ought" to have more than reasonable love for your body, or that you "ought" in any respect to do or act differently from your deeds, acts and thoughts as they are at present. Regarding others, "ought " is a word and idea with which we have nothing to do. There is no reason in saying to a blind man: "You ought to see." There is no more reason in saying to anyone: " You ought not to have this or that defect of character." Whatever our mental condition may be at present, that we must act out. A man cannot, of his individual self, put an atom more of the element of love in himself than he now has. Only the Infinite Mind can do that. Whatever of in character and belief we have today, we shall act out today in thought or deed. But we need not always have that mind.

The Overruling Mind will, as we demand, give us new minds, new truths, new beliefs, and as these supplant and drive out old errors there will come corresponding changes for the better, in both mind and body. And these ever-improving changes have no end. There is to these changes but one gate, as there is but one road. That gate and road lie in an unceasing demand of the Infinite to perfect us in Its way.

"There is a natural body, and there is a spiritual body." In other words, we have a body of physical element which can be seen and felt, and we have another body which is intangible to our physical senses. When we are able to love, cherish and admire our physical body as one piece of God's handiwork, we are putting such higher love-element not only into that physical body but also into the spiritual body. We cannot of ourselves make this quality of love. It can come to us only through demand of the Infinite. It is not vanity or that lower pride which values more whatever effect its own grace and beauty may have on others than it values that grace and beauty. The higher love for the body will attend as carefully to its external adornment in the solitude of the forest as it would in the crowded city. It will no more debase itself by any vulgar act in privacy than it would before a multitude.

God gives one personal beauty and symmetry in physical proportions, should not he or she, thus favored with a gift from the Supreme, admire these endowments? Is it vanity to love and seek to improve and increase any talent which we may find in ourselves? If God made man and woman " in His own image," is it an image to be loved and admired, or regarded with hatred and distrust? Why, the religious belief of less than a hundred years ago actually courted ugliness, and inferred that it was more creditable than beauty. Had some of those solemn-visaged professors been delegated to make an angel after their own ideal, they would have turned out a duplicate of themselves.

The Infinite, as we demand, will give us wisdom and light to know what we owe to ourselves. People have been over-ridden with the idea of their duties to parent, relative or friend. The road to heaven has been marked out as one full of sacrifice and self-denial for the sake of others, and of little good or pleasure for self. If Christ should be taken as an example in this respect, we find a very different course inferred. When charged with lack of attention to his mother, he asked; "Who is my mother?" When the young man pleads, as an excuse for not immediately following Christ, that filial duty demanded he should go and bury his father, the Messenger of a new and higher law said: "Let the dead bury their dead." In other words: If father or mother or sister or brother are steeped in a lifelong course of trespass and sin—if their lives have been one continual violation of spiritual law, bringing the inevitable penalty of disease and pain—if they are hardened and fossilized in their false beliefs, and regard your opinions as visionary and impractical you cannot, without injury, have fellowship with them. If you pretend for the sake of peace to agree with them, you are living a lie, and when you act or live a lie you materialize it and put it in your body, where it is a breeder of pain and unrest.

If others cannot see the law of life as clearly as you, and in their blindness go stumbling on and filling themselves with decay and disease, it is not in the line of the highest justice that you should be called on to nurse them every time that they are sick, to absorb their sick and unhealthy thought, to give them your life and vitality (for this you do when you think much of any one), and to be dragged down with them. You are not responsible for their blindness, nor can you open their eyes and make them see what is proven to you to be truth. Only the Infinite can do that. You do those who are in this lower and material current of thought no real good in ministering to them physically or spiritually. You may, having the stronger mind, bolster them up for a time, and, throwing your mind in theirs, you may give them your strength, but you cannot do this always, and when your influence is removed, as some time it must be, they will fall back to their old condition. What then have you accomplished You have taken so much force out of yourself that you owed to yourself; you have taught them to depend on you and not on what everyone must learn to depend on—the Supreme Power. Let the dead then, who are still above ground, bury their dead. Give them a thought and wish for their highest welfare whenever you do think of them, but leave them in God's care.

When you put the Higher Love into yourself —when you reserve your forces to raise yourself higher in the scale of being—when it is your aim and unceasing, silent prayer to be raised out of the current of the lower and material thought into that spiritual condition beyond the reach of physical disease—when you aspire to have every sense and faculty refined and strengthened beyond the present lot of mortals—when you begin to realize, through the proofs coming to you, that these are possibilities, then you are a real benefit to everyone. You are then proving a law. You are showing that there is a road out of the ills which afflict humanity, and when others, seeing these things evidenced in your own life, ask how you obtain them, you can reply: " I have grown, and am ever growing, into a higher and happier condition of mind and body, through knowledge of a law, and that law is as much for you to live by as for me." You may be able to say: " I believe in the existence of the Great Overruling Power which will show me ever the happier way of life as I demand wisdom of that Power. I had little faith in the existence of that Power at first, but I was prompted to pray or demand ability to see its reality. Now my faith in its reality is growing firmer."

To throw our whole being, care and thought into the welfare of others, no matter who they may be, without first asking of the Supreme if it be the wisest thing to do, is a sin, for it is an endeavor to use the forces given us by that Power as we think best. The result is damage to self and a great lessening of ability to do real good to others. Between the Supreme Mind and ourselves there should exist a love which is at once a love of ourselves and a love of that Mind. We must love what we draw from it, since what we draw and make part of self is drawn from God, and is a part of God. Every thought which we give to the Supreme Wisdom enriches us and directs us in the lasting path of happiness. Every thought which we give to others who are not actuated by the Higher Wisdom is unwisely bestowed. That Wisdom will direct our thought, love and sympathy to those on whom it can be bestowed without injury. To have our thoughts ever flowing spontaneously toward the Infinite Mind is to be one with God and a wise lover of self, as we feel ourselves more and more parts of God manifest in the flesh.

If we give sympathy and aid, material or moral, to others as they call for it, and without reservation or judgment, people will take all that we have to give and come open-mouthed for more. They will keep this up until we are exhausted. No outsider will put a limit to your giving. You must do that yourself. What is called "generous impulse" is sometimes another name for extravagance and injustice to somebody. Those who fling money to servitors and overpay largely for trifling services often owe that money to others, or they may owe it to themselves. In the really spiritual domain of being, we find this injustice perpetrated. on a still larger scale. Sympathetic natures sometimes give their whole lives to others. Giving thus their life and force to others becomes a fixed habit. They grow unable to restrain or control their sympathy. It overflows at everybody's call. They deprive themselves of things really needed and take up with the poorest in order to satisfy a mania for the squandering of time, force, effort and thought on others. A widely spread idea prevails that we can never give too much or do too much for others. It argues that salvation is more readily attained by such reckless expenditure of self than in any other way. No matter how barren it makes our lives—no matter of how much we deprive ourselves, it is to be made up to us tenfold in time.

We deem this a great mistake. We believe there is a Divine Economy which orders that when we give even our thought, we must give only as much as will really benefit others. Reckless prodigality throws dollars to children when cents would do them as much good. Reckless prodigality of sympathy (force) often gives ten times more to a person than that person can appropriate. What people cannot appropriate is lost for them, and when you have sent it once out you cannot recall it.

Undoubtedly to some, the idea of giving so much love to self will seem very cold, hard and unmerciful. Still this matter may be seen in a different light, when we find that "looking out for Number One," as directed by the Infinite, is really looking out for Number Two and is indeed the only way to permanently benefit Number Two. The gifts conferred by the Supreme Power are "perfect gifts," and a "perfect gift" once received by us goes out and benefits many others. So soon as one person on this planet receives the "perfect gift" of immortality in the flesh, involving perfect health and freedom from all pain and disease, that gift will be contagious, for health is catching as well as disease. The cornerstone of all symmetrical growth and constant increase of mental and physical power is the reservation and care of our thought-forces. This wisdom can only come as we demand it of the Supreme Power.

I am often asked: " How do you know what you assert? " Or: " Have you proved these assertions to yourself?" I know what I assert to be true, because I have seen its beneficial results as regards health and condition in life made evident. Other proofs are constantly coming. But what is clear to me is really no permanently convincing demonstration to any other person. That kind of proof you can only get from yourself and by the exercise and growth of your share of power given you by the Infinite. In the physical world we can safely accept the statement of a navigator who asserts his discovery of a new island. The island looks the same to every physical eye. But on the spiritual side of life spiritual things do not appear the same to all eyes. There are, so to speak, spiritual islands and spiritual realities which one person can see and another cannot see. You will see and get proof of these in proportion as you grow, and very possibly when you tell these things to others, they will call you a visionary, or will ascribe the material proof of such growth to some material cause. In the spiritual life every person is his or her own discoverer, and you need not be grieved if your discoveries are not believed in by others. It is not your business to argue and prove them to others. It is your business to push on, finding more and increase of your own individual happiness. Christ said to those of his time: "Though one rose from the dead you would not believe him." In this respect the world has not much changed since Christ used a material body on Earth.

The Art of Forgetting

In the chemistry of the future, thought will be recognized as substance even as the acids, oxides and all other chemicals of today.

There is no chasm betwixt what we call the material and spiritual. Both are of substance or element. They blend imperceptibly into each other. In reality the material is only a visible form of the finer elements which we call spiritual.

Our unseen and unspoken thought is ever flowing from us, an element and force, real as the stream of water which we can see, or the current of electricity which we cannot see. It blends with the thought of others, and out of such combination new qualities of thought are formed, as in the mixture of chemicals there are formed new substances.

If you send from you in thought the elements of worry, fret, hatred or grief, you are putting in action forces that are injurious to your mind and body. The power to forget implies the power of driving the unpleasant and hurtful thought or element, and bringing in its place the profitable element, to build up instead of tearing us down.

The character of thought which we think or put out affects our business favorably or unfavorably, It influences others for or against us. It is an element felt pleasantly or unpleasantly by others, inspiring them with confidence or distrust.

The prevailing state of mind, or character of thought, shapes the body and features. It makes us ugly or pleasing, attractive or repulsive to others. Our thought shapes our gestures, our mannerism, our walk. The least movement of muscle has a mood of mind, a thought, behind it. A mind always determined has always a determined walk. A mind always weak, shifting, vacillating and uncertain, makes a shuffling, shambling, uncertain gait. The spirit of determination braces every nerve and sinew; the thought-element of determination fills every muscle.

Look at the discontented, gloomy, melancholy and ill-tempered men or women, who manifest in their faces the operation of the silent force, which is their unpleasant thought, cutting, carving and shaping them to their present expression. Such people are never in good health, for that force acts on them as poison, and creates some form of disease. A persistent thought of determination on some purpose, especially if such purpose be of benefit to others as well as ourselves, will fill every nerve with strength. It is a wise selfishness that works to benefit others along with ourselves. In spirit, and in actual element, we are all united. We are forces which act and re-act on each other, for good or ill, through what ignorantly we call "empty space." There are unseen nerves extending from man to man, from being to being. Every form of life is in this sense connected together. We are all "members of one body." An evil thought or act is a pulsation of pain thrilling through myriads of organizations. The kindly thought and act have the same effect for pleasure. It is, then, a law of nature and of science that we cannot do a real good for another without doing one also to ourselves.

To grieve at any loss, be it of friend or property, weakens mind and body. It is no help to the friend grieved for. It is rather an injury; for our sad thought must reach its object, even if passed to another condition of existence, and is a source of pain to that person.

An hour of grumbling, fret, or fear, whether spoken or silent, uses up so much element or force   in making us less endurable to others, and perhaps making for us enemies. Directly or indirectly, it injures our business. Sour looks and words drive away good customers. Grumbling or hating is a use of actual element to belabor our minds. The force which we may so expend could be put to our pleasure and profit, even as the force we might use with a club to beat our own body can be employed to give us comfort and recreation.

To be able, then, to throw off (or forget) a thought or force which is injuring us, is a most important means of gaining strength of body and clearness of mind. Strength of body and clearness of mind bring success in all undertakings.

They bring also strength of spirit; and the forces of our spirits act on others whose bodies are thousands of miles distant, for our advantage or disadvantage. The reason is that there is a force belonging to all of us, separate and apart from that of the body. It is ever in action, and ever acting on others. It must be in operation at each moment, whether the body be asleep or awake. Ignorantly, unconsciously and hence unwisely used, it plunges us into mires of misery and error. Intelligently and wisely used, it will bring us every conceivable good.

That force is our thought. Every thought of ours is of vital importance to health and true success. And so-called success, as the world terms it, is not real. A fortune gained at the cost of health is not a real success.

Every mind trains itself, generally unconsciously, to its peculiar character or quality of thought. Whatever that training is, it cannot be immediately changed. We may have trained our minds unconsciously to nourish evil or troubled thought. We may never have realized that brooding over disappointment, living in a grief, dreading a loss, fretting for fear this or that might not succeed as we wish, was building up a destructive force which has bled away our strength, created disease, unfitted us for business, and caused us loss of money and possibly loss of friends.

To learn to forget is as necessary and useful as to learn to remember. We think of many things every day which it would be more profitable not to think of at all. The ability to forget is the ability to drive away the unseen force (thought) which Is injuring us, and to change it for a force (or order of thought) which can benefit us.

Demand imperiously and persistently any quality of character in which you may be lacking, and you will attract increase of such quality. Demand more patience or decision, more judgment or courage, more hopefulness or exactness, and you will increase in such qualities. These qualities are real elements. They belong to the subtler, and as yet unrecognized, chemistry of Nature.

The discouraged, hopeless and whining man has unconsciously demanded discouragement and hopelessness. So he gets it. This is his unconscious mental training for evil. Mind is "magnetic," because it attracts to itself whatever thought it fixes itself upon, or that to which it opens itself. Give space to fear, and you will fear more and more. Cease to resist its tendency, make no effort to forget it, and you open the door and invite fear in; you then demand fear. Set your mind on the thought of courage, see yourself in mind or imagination as courageous, and you will become more stout of heart. You demand courage.

There is no limit in unseen nature to the supply of these spiritual qualities. In the words: "Ask and ye shall receive," the Christ implied that any mind could, through demanding, draw to itself all that it needed of any quality. Demand wisely, and we draw to us the best.

Every second of wise demand brings an increase of power. Such increase is never lost to us. This is an effort for lasting gain that we can use at any time. What all of us want is more power to work results, and build up our fortunes,—power to make things about us more comfortable, to ourselves and our friends. We cannot feed others if we have no energy to keep starvation from ourselves. The power to do this is a different thing from the power to hold in memory other people's opinions, or a collection of so-called facts gathered from books, which time often proves to be fictions. Every success in any grade of life has been accomplished through spiritual power, through unseen force flowing from one mind, working on other minds far and near, and as real as the force in your arm which lifts a stone.

A man may be illiterate, yet he may send from his mind a force affecting and influencing many others, far and near, in a way to benefit his fortunes, while the scholarly man drudges with his brain on a pittance. The illiterate man's is then a greater spiritual power. Intellect is not a bag to hold facts. Intellect is power to work results. Writing books is but a fragment of the work of intellect. The greatest philosophers have planned first, and acted afterwards, as did Columbus, Napoleon, Fulton, Morse, Edison and others, who have moved the world, besides telling the world how it should be moved.

Your plan, purpose or design, whether relating to a business or an invention, is a real construction of unseen thought-element. Such thought-structure is also a magnet. It commences to draw aiding forces to it so soon as made. Persist in holding to your plan or purpose, and these forces come nearer and nearer; they become stronger and stronger, and will bring more and more favorable results.

Abandon your purpose, and you stop the further approach of these forces, destroying also so much of unseen attracting power as you have already built up. Success in any business depends on the application of this law. Persistent resolve on any purpose is a real attractive force or element, drawing constantly more and more aids for carrying out that resolve.

When your body is in the state called sleep, these forces (your thoughts) are still active. They are then working on other minds. If your last thought before sleep is that of worry, of anxiety, of hatred for anyone, it will work for you only ill results. If it is hopeful, cheerful, confident and at peace with all men, it is then the stronger force, and will work for you good results. If the sun goes down on your anger, that wrathful thought will act on others, while you sleep, and bring only injury in return.

Is it not a necessity, then, to cultivate the power of forgetting what we wish, so that the current which attracts the ill, while our body rests, shall be changed to the current which attracts the good alone? Today thousands on thousands never think of controlling the character of their thought. They allow their minds to drift. They never say of a thought that is troubling them: "I won't think of it." Unconsciously then they demand what works them ill, and their bodies are made sick by the kind of thought on which they allow their minds to fasten.

When you realize the injury done you through any kind of troubled thought, you will then commence to acquire the power of casting it aside. When in mind you commence to resist such injurious thought, you are constantly gaining more and more power for resistance. "Resist the devil," said the Christ, " and he will flee from you." There are no devils save the ill-used forces of the mind. But these are most powerful to afflict and torture us. An ugly or melancholy mood of mind is a devil. It can make us sick, lose us friends, and lose us money. Money means the enjoyment of necessities and comforts. Without these we cannot do or be our best. The sin involved in " love of money" is to love money better than the things needful which money can bring.

To bring to us the greatest success in any business, to make the greatest advance in any art, to further any cause, it is absolutely necessary that at certain daily intervals we should forget all about that business, art or cause. By so doing we rest our minds, and gather fresh force for renewed effort.

To be ever revolving the same plan, study or speculation, what we shall do or shall not do, is to waste such force on a brain-treadmill. We are in thought saying to ourselves the same thing over and over again. We are building of this actual, unseen element, of this thought, the same constructions over and over again. One is a useless duplicate of the other.

If we are always inclined to think or converse on one particular subject; if we will never forget it; if we will start it at all times and in all places; if we will not in thought and speech fall into the prevailing tone of the conversation about us; if we do not try to get up an interest in what is being talked of by others; if we determine only to converse on what interests us, or not converse at all, we are in danger of becoming "cranks" or monomaniacs.

The "crank" draws his reputation on himself. He is one who, having forced one idea, and one alone, on himself, has resolved, perhaps unconsciously, to foist that same idea on everybody else. He will not forget at periods his pet theory or purpose, and adapt himself to the height of others. For this reason he loses the power to forget, to throw from his mind the one absorbing thought. He drifts more and more into that one idea. He surrounds himself with its peculiar atmosphere, or element, and it becomes no less real than any other which we can see or handle.

Others near him feel the influence of this single idea, and feel it disagreeably, because the thought of one person is felt by others near him through a sense as yet unnamed. In the exercise of this sense lies the secret of your favorable or unfavorable "impressions" of people at first sight. You are in thought, as it flows from you always, sending into the air an element which affects others for or against you, according to its quality, and in proportion to the acuteness of their sense which feels thought. You are influenced by the thought of others in the same way, be they far or near. Hence we are talking to others when our tongues are still. We are making ourselves hated or loved while we sit alone in the privacy of our chambers.

A crank often becomes a martyr, or thinks himself one. There is no absolute necessity for martyrdom in any cause, save the necessity of ignorance. There never was any absolute necessity, save for the same reason. Martyrdom always implies lack of judgment and tact in the presentation of any principle new to the world. Analyze martyrdom, and you will find in the martyr a determination to force on people some idea in an offensive and antagonistic form. People of great ability, through dwelling on one idea, have at last been captured by it. The antagonism which they drew from others they drew because they held it first in their own mind.

"I come not to bring peace," said the Christ, "but a sword." The time has now come in the world's history for the sword to be sheathed. Many good people unconsciously use swords in advising what they deem better things. There is the sword (in thought) of the scolding reformer, the sword of dislike for others because they won't heed what you say, and the sword of prejudice because others won't adopt your peculiar habits. Every discordant thought against others is a sword, and calls out from others a sword in return. The thought which you thus put forth is the thought that you receive back, and it is therefore after the same kind.

The coming empire of peace is to be built up by reconciling differences, making friends of enemies, telling people of the good that is in them rather than the bad, discouraging gossip and evil-speaking by the introduction of subjects more pleasant and profitable, and proving through one's life that there are laws, not generally recognized, which will give health, happiness and fortune, without injustice or injury to others. Its advocate will meet the sick with the smile of true friendship, for the most diseased people are always the greatest sinners. The most repulsive man or woman, the creature full of deceit, treachery and venom, needs your pity and help of all the most, for that man or woman, through generating evil thought, is generating pain and disease for himself or for herself.

You are thinking of a person unpleasantly from whom you have received some slight or insult, an injury or injustice. Such thought remains with you hour after hour, perhaps day after day. You become at last tired of it, yet cannot throw it off. It annoys, worries, frets, sickens you. You cannot prevent yourself from going round on this same tiresome, troublesome track of thought. It wears out your spirit; and whatever wears the spirit, wears also the body.

This is because you have drawn on yourself the other person's opposing and hostile thought. He is thinking of you, as you are of him. He is sending you a wave of hostile thought. You are both giving and receiving the blows of unseen elements. You may keep up this silent war of unseen force for weeks and, if so, both are injured. This contest of opposing wills and forces is going on all about us. The air is full of it.

The struggle to forget enemies, or to throw out to them only friendly thought, is then as much an act of serf-protection as to put up your hands and ward off a physical blow. The persistent thought of friendliness turns aside thought of ill-will, and renders it harmless. The injunction of Christ to do good to your enemies is founded on a natural law. It is saying that the thought or element of good will carries the greater power, and will always turn aside and prevent injury coming from the thought of ill-will.

Demand forgetfulness when you can only think of a person or of anything with the pain that comes of grief, anger or any other cause. Demand is a state of mind which sets in motion forces to bring you the result needed. Demand is the scientific basis of prayer. Do not supplicate. Demand persistently your share of force out of the elements about you, by which you can rule your mind to any desired mood.

There are no limits to the strength which may be gained through the cultivation of our thought- power. It can keep from us all pain arising from grief, from loss of fortune, loss of friends, and disagreeable situations in life. Such power is the very element or attitude of mind most favorable to the gain of fortune and friends. The stronger mind throws off the burdensome, wearying, fretting thought, forgets it, and interests itself in something else. The weaker mind dwells in the fretting, worrying thought, and is enslaved thereby. When you fear a misfortune (which may never happen), your body becomes weak; your energy is paralyzed. But you can, through constantly demanding it, dig out of yourself a power which will throw off any fear or troublesome state of mind. Such power is the high road to success.

Demand it, and it will increase more and more, until at last you will know no fear. A fearless man or woman can accomplish wonders.

That no individual may have gained the full height of this power, is no proof that it cannot be really gained. Newer and more wonderful things are ever happening in the world. Some decades ago, and he who should assert that a human voice could be heard between New York and Philadelphia would have been called a lunatic. Now, the wonder of the telephone is an everyday affair. The powers, still unrecognized, of our thought will make the telephone of trivial importance. Men and women, through cultivation and use of this power, are to do wonders which fiction dares not or has not put before the world.

Spells; Or, the Law of Change

A condition of mind can be brought on you, resulting to you in good or ill, sickness or health, wealth or poverty, by the action, conscious or unconscious, of other minds about you, and also through the thought suggested to you by objects or scenes about you.

This is the secret of what in former times was called the "spell." Through the action of thought a state of mind can be brought on any person which may make them act conformably to such thought.

The "spell" is a matter of everyday occurrence in some form or other. To remain for an hour in sight of grand scenery casts on the mind a "spell" of pleasurable thought. To remain for an hour in a vault surrounded by coffins and skeletons would, through the associations connected with such objects, cast on you a "spell" of gloom. To live for days and weeks in a family, all of whose members hated you, or were prejudiced against you, would most likely cast on you a spell of depression and unpleasant sensation. To live in a family whose members were always sending you warm and friendly thought would produce a " spell" of pleasurable sensation.

If, when sick, you are obliged to remain for days and possibly weeks in the same room, your mind will become weary of seeing continually the same objects in it. Not only is the mind wearied at sight of these objects, but the sight of each one, from day to day, will suggest the same train of thoughts. which also soon becomes wearisome. Mind weariness, from this or any other cause, has a natural drift towards despondency. Matters present and future then assume their darkest aspect and the darkest side of every possibility comes uppermost. Despondent thought, as has been many times repeated, is force used to tear the body down instead of building it up.

This action and condition of thought is one form of the "spell." It is broken most speedily by a change to another place and another room.

For this reason "change of scene" is frequently recommended to the invalid. Change of scene and locality means not only a change of objects beheld by the eye but a change also in thought, as new ideas, and possibly a new condition of mind, come through seeing the new set of objects. The new condition of mind will "break the spell."

There is a much closer connection between things tangible and seen of the eye and things intangible than is generally imagined. In other words, there is a close connection between things material and thing spiritual.

The force or element which we call " thought" is all-pervading, and takes innumerable varieties of expression. A tree is an expression of thought as well as a man, and so are all that we call inanimate objects.

There is not a thoroughly dead or inanimate thing in the universe, but there are countless shades of life or animation. Many things seem dead to us, as a bone or a stone, but there is a life or force which has built that bone or stone into its present condition, and that same life or force, after that bone or stone has served a certain purpose, will take it to pieces again and build its elements into other forms. The unbuilding process we call decomposition. It matters not if the stone change or rid itself of but one atom in a thousand years. Time is nothing in the working of Nature's forces. Decomposition, then, is a proof of the existence of all-pervading and ever-working life or force. Otherwise, the stone or bone would remain without change through all Eternity. Incessant change is ever going on in the boundless universe; it is an Inevitable accompaniment of all life; and the greater the life and force in you, the more rapid and varied will be the changes.

Everything, from a stone to a human being, sends out to you, as you look upon it, a certain amount of force, affecting you beneficially or injuriously according to the quantity of life or animation which it possesses.

Take any article of furniture, a chair or bedstead, for instance. It contains not only the thought of those who first planned and molded it in its construction, but it is also permeated with the thought and varying moods of all who have sat on it or slept in it. So also are the walls and every article of furniture in any room permeated with the thought of those who have dwelt in it, and if it has been long lived in by people whose lives were narrow, whose occupation varied little from year to year, whose moods were dismal and cheerless, the walls and furniture will be saturated with this gloomy and sickly order of thought.

If you are very sensitive, and stay in such a room but for a single day, you will feel in some way the depressing effect of such thought, unless you keep very positive to it, and to keep sufficiently positive for twenty-four hours at a time to resist it would be extremely difficult. If you are in any degree weak or ailing you are then most negative or open to the nearest thought- element about you, and will be affected by it, in addition to the wearying mental effect, first mentioned, of any object kept constantly before the eyes.

It is injurious, then, to be sick, or even wearied, in a room where other people have been sick, or where they have died, because in thought-element all the misery and depression, not only of the sick and dying but of such as gathered there and sympathized with the patient, will be still left in that room, and this is a powerful unseen agent for acting injuriously on the living.

Those "simple savages" who after a death burn not only the habitation but every article used by the deceased when alive, may know more of Nature's injurious and beneficial forces than we know. Living more natural lives, they unconsciously act according to the law, even as animals in their wild and natural state do, thereby escaping many of the pains and discomforts of the artificial life which we have made both for ourselves and the animals that we domesticate.

People who have some purpose in life, who travel a great deal, who are ever on the move and in contact with different persons and places, have, you will notice, more vitality, more energy, and physically preserve a certain freshness not evident with those who follow year after year an unvarying round of occupation, carrying them day after day to one certain locality, whether office or desk or workman's bench, just as a pendulum oscillates from side to side.

These last look older at forty than the active, changing person does at sixty, because their unvarying lives, the daily presence and sight of the same objects at their dwellings or places of business, contact with the same individual or individuals at meals and in leisure moments, and interchange of about the same thoughts year in and year out, weave about them an invisible web composed of strands or filaments of the same unvarying thought, and this web literally strengthens from year to year, exactly as strand after strand of wire laid together will form at last the massive bridge-supporting cable. But the unseen cable so made binds people more and more firmly to the same place, the same occupation, and the same unvarying set of habits. It makes them dislike more and more even the thought of any change. It is another form of the "spell" which they have woven for themselves. It is the sure result of always keeping your state of mind unchanged.

We do not live on bread or meat alone. We live also largely on ideas. The person ever planning and moving new enterprises, the person who throws his force into beneficial public movements, and from either of these causes is led into a varied and ever-changing contact with individuals, receives and puts out a far greater variety of thought than the man who lives continually in a nutshell.

There is a time and use for retirement and solitude. There is a time and use for contact with the world. It is desirable to establish the golden mean between the two.

The person whose range of life and movement is narrow, who is doing nearly the same thing and seeing nearly the same things and people from year to year, has a tendency to feed mostly on the same old set of thoughts and ideas. Out of himself he generates the same order of old, stale notion and expression. Start him in a certain train of idea or association and he tells you time after time the same old story, forgetting how many times he has told it you before. He has about the same forms of expression for every occurrence and every hour of the day. He regards the world and things generally as about worn out. Lacking in life and variety of thought himself, he regards everything else as lacking in life and variety. For life is to us exactly as we see it through the spectacles which we so often unconsciously make to look at it. If our mental spectacles, through living unaware in violation of the Law, are blurred, cracked, discolored, and dim, the whole world will to us seem blurred, discolored, and dull in hue.

Such a person "ages," as we term it, very rapidly, because his physical body is as much an expression of his daily and prevailing order of thought as the apple is an expression or part of the apple tree. Feeding and living on the same set of ideas continually is analogous fo feeding continually on a most limited variety of food. Both bring on disease. In some of the English prisons what are called "oatmeal sores" afflict the prisoners through being fed so much on that single article.

But the average mental condition shows itself on the body far more rapidly than any result from material diet. It is feeding on the same stale set of ideas, aided by living continually amid the same physical surroundings and with the same individuals, who are likewise subsisting mentally on the same stale mental diet, that whitens the hair, stoops the shoulders, wrinkles the face, and causes shrinkage of tissues and bodily inertia and weakness. Our land is full of people who at forty-five, through this cause, look older than others of sixty-five. It is full also of young men and women in a physical sense, who, through their poverty of idea and lack of real life, will be old, worn, and haggard within twenty years. They are in substance as much old fogies, "grannies," and "daddies" now as are those whom they ridicule as such. They are traveling in the same narrow rut of idea. Slang phrases and worn-out chaff, borrowed from others, constitute four- fifths of their talk and probably five-sixths of their thought.

To this class also belong many who are deemed of a high order intellectually, or of more "culture," whose thought after all is very largely a repetition of what they have heard or read, who look up to and idolize some human authority, living or dead, and have really very few ideas of their own, not possibly because new ideas occasionally do not suggest themselves to them, but they have not the courage to secretly entertain and familiarize themselves with such ideas. They smother them. They succeed at last in killing them and putting out the little light endeavoring to shine on them. When you destroy or so kill out of yourself the capacity for truthful idea to act upon you, you are killing also your body by degrees. You are cutting off the only source of new life for the body.

Of this order of minds the only claim to youth lies in that physical freshness belonging to the earlier growth and life of the body, which, owing to their mental condition, will fade in twenty years as surely as the absence of sunshine and water will soon wither the young and growing plant.

Such are now unconsciously weaving for themselves the web and "spell" of age and decay.

A constant renewal of physical life lies only in a never-ceasing change of mental conditions. New ideas beget newer and fresher views of life. There are millions on millions of truthful, new ideas ready to come to us, provided we keep the mind in the proper state to receive them. We have not to plod and "study hard" to receive them. There is no "hard study" in the kingdom of God or the kingdom of infinite good. If in the line of communication with that kingdom, we shall ever receive new thought, as the plant receives the sunshine and air, and like the plant just as much as suffices to give us life for the day and the hour. Every mind is now, or is to be at some period of its existence (not possibly in this present physical existence), a fountain for the reception of such new idea.

But new thought cannot come from books or from the ideas of others. These may for a time serve to start you on the road, or as temporary props or helps. But if you depend altogether on books or people for new thought, you are living on borrowed life. You, in so doing, keep your own mind closed to the inflowing of the element which its own individual needs call for, which is for it alone and for no other mind. You must draw your own sustenance from the infinite reservoir of truthful thought. Until you do so you are not a "well of water springing up into everlasting life," nor have you reached the initial point of that real and perfected existence which feels at home anywhere in the universe and can draw its self-sustaining life at any place in the universe.

No agency fetters more or does more harm to both mind and body than a very close and constant association with a mind or minds inferior to yours in tastes, in refinement, in breadth of views and quality of motive.

Such order of mind ever near you and with which you are much in sympathy, will infuse into yours more or less of its grosser desire or taste. It will blind you more or less to higher and healthier views and modes of life. You will, unconsciously to yourself, live and act out much of that mind's life. You will be peevish or cynical or mean in your dealings, when it is not the real you that is so thinking or acting, but the constant flow to you and reception by you of the grosser force or element of that mind, which you thus act out. You become, then, literally a part of the other and inferior mind. This will surely affect the body which in its material substance becomes a material expression of that lower mind grafted on yours. Unless you sunder this mental tie, the inferior graft may outgrow the original tree. You will become physically inert, lifeless, and be affected with some form of disease, because you are then giving that inferior graft your own thought or force. It can appropriate but a small part of that force, but from what it can, it draws its own stinted life. You are then giving of your gold and getting base metal in return. You are then giving of your life and getting a slow and living death in return. For the mind most clear and active in thought, considerate, wise and prudent, broadly but not recklessly benevolent in action, does give to others, and especially to those with whom it is in close sympathy, life and vigor, both of mind and body.

Talking openly has very little to do with the good or ill results coming of minds in close association and sympathy. It is not what people talk. It is what people think of each other that most affects them. A person always near you and ever thinking of you with dissatisfaction or peevishness, or putting out the thought of opposition to your aims and wishes, will eventually make you feel unpleasantly, be his or her words ever so fair. Such a person, under these circumstances, will at last injure you in mind and body. That person is throwing a "spell" on you.

On the contrary, the near presence of a person pleasantly disposed toward you, who wishes to bring you pleasure or benefit without "an axe to grind," will give you a feeling of rest and quiet, though such person may not say a word for hours. These different sensations are among the many proofs that thought is a literal element, in some way ever affecting us, and ever bringing results as it comes to us from others or is sent by us to others. In this last case the "spell" may be beneficial to you.

There is but one way of breaking the evil spell caused by continual association with the inferior mind or minds, which spell will surely prove fatal if continued in, and is indeed proving fatal to thousands at the present day. That method is an entire separation from such mind or minds.

Such sundering of these injurious mental ties cannot, however, in every case be abrupt, or evils may result as great as those which it is sought to avoid. If a graft, however injurious, be roughly torn from the tree, the tree also is injured and perhaps destroyed. If your life has been one of long association with a lower mind, if both of you have, as previously stated, grown into a common life, and you are suddenly torn apart, the shock may prove to you injurious.

If one subsists for a long time on an injurious food, still a certain kind of life is derived from that food, and as the system has become accustomed to it, it cannot be immediately replaced by a healthier food. The system at first may not be able thoroughly to assimilate and digest such healthier food. There is a similar action and result as regards our mental diet.

Once be convinced of the evil resulting to you from any close, inferior association, and you will first assume in mind that such tie must be sundered. Assume this persistently. and half the work is done. That changed state of mind is the force then always working to free you, as your former state of mind, which endured, suffered, and submitted internally, was the force which bound you more and more firmly. The separation is now in your changed mental attitude simply a work of time. You have little to do, save to walk and take advantage of opportunities as they offer themselves. You have, in fact, committed yourself to another current of thought, and the forces coming of your changed mental condition and interior resolve are the spiritual correspondence of a great river to whose current you have committed yourself, and it is slowly bearing you away from your former enslaved condition. This is not a figurative illustration; change permanently a state of mind in which you have been for years; change unwilling submission into a hidden resolve no longer to submit; change endurance of near associations into a permanent and hidden resolve that you will separate from such associations; change that enforced content called "resignation to circumstances," as, for instance, resignation to the presence of inferior, squalid, and unpleasant material surroundings, into that positive internal mental attitude, which in plain language says—"I won't put up with this any longer; my body may be obliged to submit, endure, and suffer from these things temporarily, as it has done in the past, but in mind I will neither endure nor be resigned as I have been "—and you have placed yourself in the action of another power which will gradually bear you away from the old source of ill.

It is not so much what we do as what we think that brings results. By the force put out of what you permanently think are you carried, as on a current, to those results. You need do very little until you see that the time and opportunity has come for doing. It would be poor judgment for a man floating on a log down the Mississippi to keep on splashing the water and thereby using up his strength for the sake of "doing something." He had better remain quiet and take the chances of being picked up by a passing boat or steamer, or wait until he sees an opportunity of catching on to some near projecting headland. Then such strength as he may have been able to reserve will be used to some purpose. When you are in the right current of thought, you need in similar manner to reserve your strength until you meet the opportunity which that current will bring you, for as many injured through unwise and overmuch doing as by too little. If you don't know what to do, wait. When you wait till your hurry is over, you may see what really needs to be done.

Above all things, in any emergency or experience such as is suggested here, demand daily and hourly in silent thought the aid of a Higher Wisdom and Divine Power. There must come response to such demand. I do not assume to lay down a certain unbending rule to govern every individual life. Every individual life, when it places itself in the line of communication with its Higher Wisdom through a persistent mental attitude, asking silently for such wisdom, will make its own methods for riddance of the ills from which it desires to free itself, and such methods belong to it individually, nor can they safely be copied and used by anyone else. The Spirit of Infinite Good does not reveal itself alike to any two persons. The besetting error of our time is to copy or imitate other people's methods in everything, or to become blindly obedient to a book or the mind that wrote a book. Your mind, ever asking for Wisdom and Truth, is a power beyond any book and is now, or is to be, the reservoir into which ideas will flow which are different from those contained in any book. The power which generates and suggests new ideas is ever coming to the world. The book does not advance after it is written. But the mind which put ideas in that book may be ever going ahead and finding new meanings and broader interpretations for what it wrote years before.

If you wish to find out regarding the latest developments in chemistry or any material science, you do not have recourse to the books written a hundred years ago about such matters. You get the latest work on these subjects, and if possible you will go farther and get access to those now making such sciences their special studies, seeing that they may know something regarding them never yet written.

So even now in your own kingdom of mind there may be ideas and truths beyond any ever written, which you reject as "mere imaginings," or dare not assert either by word or act for fear of ridicule or opposition.

A book, like Paul, may plant new ideas in your mind; an individual like Apollos "may water" such ideas, but the awakened God in yourself can alone give the increase.

Complete isolation from their kind and loneliness is one terrible fear besetting some who live in associations which are really not congenial to them, but from which they dare not separate for fear of that loneliness. Try not to fear this. Permanent solitude is not in the order of Nature for anyone. Minds alike in thought were made to mingle and give each other pleasure. It is often the clinging to that order of association which, after all, only wearies you, and may oblige you often to play an enforced part to meet such association, that forms the barrier keeping you from your real companions. So long as (in mind) you accept the lower association, so long are you keeping the better away and sending it farther from you. So soon as you reject the lower (in mind), so soon do you set in motion the force to bring the better to you.

REGENERATION; OR, BEING BORN AGAIN

We do not yet know the full meaning or value of life.

The commonly held idea of existence runs thus: to be born, to grow from infancy to youth, from youth to maturity, from maturity to old age, from old age to death. During these stages, to gain possibly fame or fortune, but ever at the end to weaken, sicken, and die.

Man's real and ever-growing life is a condition so unlike this present existence, that there is scarcely a possibility of any realization thereof by comparison between the two. If you had never seen anything of a tree but its roots in the dark, damp ground, could anyone by means of words convey to you a realization of the beauty of its foliage and blossoms in the sunlight?

Our physical existence is the root from which in the future is to come an indescribable beauty and power.

Some speak lightly of their bodies, call them encumbrances, and entertain glowing anticipations, when rid of them, of a blissful life, entirely in the spiritual realm of existence.

This involves an error.

Because a certain physical life with ever-refining physical senses is in every stage of existence a necessity to the fullest completement of our lives.

The Christ of Judea spoke of the necessity of "Regeneration." "Ye must be born again," he Says.

Reincarnated we all have been many times. Regeneration is a step beyond reincarnation.

Reincarnation means the total loss of one physical body and the getting of a new one through the aid of another organization. Regeneration means the perpetuation of an ever refining physical body without that total separation of spirit and body called death.

The cruder the spirit, the longer were the intervals of time between its getting for itself a new physical body through reincarnation.

As the spirit was quickened and gained power, these intervals became less in duration, numbering years in place of centuries. With still greater increase of power the spirit will seek the regenerative instead of the reincarnative process of perpetuating its life of the physical senses.

A spiritualizing and refining power has ever been and ever will be working on this planet. It has through innumerable ages changed all forms of being, whether mineral, animal, or vegetable, from coarse to finer types. It works with man as with all other organizations. It is ever changing him gradually from a material to a more spiritual being. It is carrying him through his many physical existence from one degree of perfection to another. It has in store for him new powers, new lives, and new methods of existence. That spiritual power has given him in the past new inventions. It illuminated his mind to see the uses of steam, electricity, and other material agencies. But far greater illumination is to come. A time is coming when he will not need iron, steam, and electricity to promote his convenience or enjoyment. New powers born out of his spiritual life will supersede the necessity of many of his present material aids.

There will come in the future a more perfected life, when, for the few at first and the many afterwards, there will be no physical death. In other words, every spirit will be able to use both its spiritual and physical senses, through the continual regeneration of its physical body.

Such making over and over again of the physical body will come of successive changes of mind. There will be continual separations from one old state of mind after another and entrances into new. We shall ever through regeneration be born into new individualities.

Regeneration may supersede reincarnation, because of our coming into a higher order of life, or receiving and being built of a higher order of thoughts. The spirit will then be ever changing its physical body for one still finer and more spiritualized. This is the process referred to by Christ as being "born again."

Life is an eternal series of regenerations. The whole aim and scope of all these writings is the endeavor to show what life really means; how the spiritual life rules the physical life; and how we are all growing from cruder to finer forms of life.

The spirit is regenerated when it shakes off the old physical body. It shakes off an old body because it is tired of carrying an instrument through which it cannot express itself. The old man or woman of decaying powers has as much mind or spirit as ever. But that mind cannot act on its body. It is cut off in a sense from that body. It is receding from that body and will finally quit it altogether. It recedes because, through ignorance, it has been drawing for years inferior thought and a monotonous round of thought to the body and endeavoring to make it over again with an old rotten material. It is like trying to repair a leaky roof with rotten shingles. This is the degenerative process of today and the cause of the decaying physical powers and death of the body.

But the more enlightened spirit will find out how to act on and replenish the body with newer and newer thought. This makes the body ever newer and newer and so keeps up the necessary connection between spirit and body.

We do not part with life in the loss of the physical body. But we do lose thereby one kind of life and a most important agency for the fullest enjoyment of life.

We lose in what is called death the use of that set of senses which we call the physical. We lose the power of living in a close connection with the world of physical things. It is most desirable to maintain a connection with the physical world, and the spirit on losing its body, contrary to general belief, laments the loss of such body and desires eagerly to have the possession and use of its former physical senses. Failing in this it uses, so far as it can. by a psychological law, the physical senses of those having bodies, whom it can influence or control.

Every living man and woman has such influence brought to bear on him or her from the unseen side of life.

The "dead," as they are falsely called, resume imperfectly their lives on earth, through aid unconsciously given them by the living, or, more properly speaking, by those living with physical bodies.

If we do not wish to find out the new—if we instantly reject what some may call "new-fangled ideas"—if we want to go on in the old way of our fathers, then we invite the company and mind of spirits as ignorant as ourselves, who will only help on the decay of our bodies after getting from them all the use they can.

These are "unregenerated spirits." They have drawn to them little new thought since losing their bodies. They will by reason of the same ignorance through which they lost the last physical body, be drawn into another reincarnation, and perhaps another and another, until at last, gaining with each life more knowledge, they will know how to regenerate their bodies.

This regeneration will not come of any material medicines or methods. It will come of changing spiritual conditions. These spiritual conditions will cause the adoption of new habits and ways of life. But to adopt these habits before the spiritual condition prompts or demands them will do little good.

We have a life of the physical senses. We have another of the finer or spiritual senses. We live during the waking hours by the physical senses. We live another life during sleep by the spiritual senses. When these two lives are properly adjusted, they feed each other healthfully.

With such proper adjustment the physical senses receive a certain necessary supply of element from the spiritual while the body sleeps.

The spiritual being receives also from the material condition a certain vital supply. If your spirit loses its body these sources of mutual supply between body and spirit are for a time cut off.

The more perfected or regenerated life of the future means the consciousness of existence by both the physical and spiritual senses.

The life of the physical senses and that of the spiritual senses are necessary to each other. When they are joined together, and we become conscious of the use of both, life is relatively perfected and the spirit attains a degree of happiness not now to be imagined.

During all the centuries which have passed since Christ's time, can we point to any instance of this new birth or regeneration? If such regeneration is owing to a higher Faith and higher Law, can we say that any persons, no matter what may have been their reputation for piety or uprightness, whose bodies have finally sickened and decayed, have lived up to the highest Law?

"The wages of sin is death," says the Bible. We would prefer to say that the result of an unperfected life is the death of the physical body.

The body of every weak, shriveled, trembling old man or woman today is the result of sins committed in ignorance. Those sins lay in their thoughts. Out of such thought as it attracts the spirit builds first its spiritual body. The physical body is a material correspondence of the spiritual body. If the spirit believes in error it builds that error into the body. The result is decay.

For this result no blame can be imputed to those who suffer. They have lived up to all the light and knowledge they had. With more growth there will, in some condition of existence, come to them more knowledge. They will then see new methods of living and avoid the mistakes of the former less perfected life.

Charity comes of the knowledge that all people live up to the best light which they have. God alone can light up the darkened chambers of our and their minds. When we, leaving the faults of others alone, ask that our minds may be illuminated so as to see and avoid evil, that illumination alone will help all about us.

People weary of existence, because they think year after year the same set of thoughts and ideas over and over again. Eternal life and happiness come of a perpetual flow to us of new thought and idea. Thought is food for our spiritual beings. Our physical bodies are not nourished on one monotonous kind of food from year to year. Feed the spirit with the same thought (or try to) from year to year and it becomes sick. The sick spirit makes the sick body.

The Law of Eternal Life will not allow this repetition to go on. The Law says to us: "You were not made to run in ruts and grooves of fixed habit. You are not as John Smith or John Brown to be an eternal individuality without change, like a post rooted in the ground. You are to have a new mind for this period, and a superior mind with increased Powers of perception for the next period. You are ever, by drawing to you and adding to you new thought, to be as so many different individuals; as you live on, and this process of regeneration proceeds, you are born or changed into successive types of being, each one being finer than the last."

The regenerated life with a physical body means an ever-increasing life. It means a fresher capacity, with each day's waking, to sense that beauty in Nature which exists all around us. It means a new glory in each day's sunshine. It means a repose and restfulness whereby we can sit still and feel the spirit which animates the tree, the leaf, the ocean, the rivulet, the star, the flower, and every natural expression of the Infinite Mind. It means the daily flow to us of new thoughts which shall fill us with new life. It means that we shall rejoice in the realization and firmly grounded faith that we have in us the possibilities for development into numberless new lives. It means that power of so losing our material self in any effort which we may make that all sense of time shall vanish and ennui and mental weariness shall be destroyed. It means power to live without drudgery of mind and body, or that anxiety which is even worse than drudgery. It means at last the getting of enjoyment from all things. To get enjoyment from everything Is to get life from everything. To get life from everything is to get power from all things. To get power implies a control of all physical elements. This includes a power of ever holding an ever-refining physical body.

Ennui is sickness. When we don't know what to do with ourselves, when we try to kill time and everything seems " flat, stale and unprofitable, we have temporarily lost our hold of the Great Fountain of life, the Supreme Mind and Power. We are absorbing the wearied thoughts of thousands around us, who think the same thing from day to day and from year to year, whose minds in their play are treadmills, who are trying to get Life, exhilaration and variety entirely out of physical things.

The true and regenerative life cannot be obtained from material things. That is the reason why all that money can buy fails to satisfy. The monster of discontent and ennui rages as much in the palace as the hovel. Solomon was in the claws of this beast when he said: "Vanity of vanities, all is vanity." That exclamation is a libel on the Infinite Mind. It came from the Jewish king, because he was trying to get life and happiness out of wood and stone and metal, and flesh and blood and all things material. It cannot be done.

But when, through demand of the Supreme, you get new thoughts, the material thing of yesterday seems to you as a new thing of today. The very rock which you passed yesterday has a new idea associated with it today. It may not be an idea which you can put in words. It is something which you feel rather than think. Myriads of thoughts, coming at the physical sight of all material things about us, are so felt, but can neither be talked out nor written out.

The regeneration of the body comes in response to our increasing demand of the Supreme Power to be led in the path of the Highest Wisdom. It comes of a courage gained at last of persistent demand, whereby we shall dare to trust entirely to that power. This it is doubtful if any can do at present. We try to trust in God, but when the pinch comes and things look dark, we are tempted to adopt some of our worn-out material methods for averting the evil. But perfect trust in the Supreme Power can gradually come to us. When it does men will become more than mortal. Whoever attains to such perfect trust will be regenerated.

Demand then new thoughts, and an increasing nearness to the Supreme Mind, and in time you receive new life, and all things about you are, for you, imbued with new life or idea. You are then in the line of the regenerative process. Your spirit, as well as your body, is being born again and again. It is drawing to it ever new ideas, and becomes literally a new spirit, a new being. If the spirit is being thus renewed or regenerated, the body must be also.

As we become more spiritualized, as the material mind gives place more and more to the Spiritual Mind; in other words, as the regenerative process goes on, we shall, from time to time, find ourselves prompted to change many of our habits and modes of life. These changes will involve eating, sleeping, and association.

But we need not try to force these changes on ourselves. The regenerative process will involve the eating of less and less animal food, until we shall eat none whatever. But there would be nothing gained from ceasing to eat meat before the desire for It had gone.

The regenerative process will impel us at times to seek solitude, because when alone with Nature the spirit absorbs and assimilates a finer quality of thought. But to enforce on ourselves the solitude of the hermitage or cloister when there is no real love for it does little good, as is proved by the fact that hermit and recluse have physically decayed and died like the rest.

This regeneration of the body will come to no one directly from any system of forms, habits, or observances. It will come because of a time ripe for it to come. As this planet ripens spiritually all material things upon it partake of that ripening or development. The life of today, so different and superior to that of five hundred or a thousand years ago, is a part and a proof of that development. The earth ripened first from chaos to coarse development in the animal and vegetable kingdoms of ages ago, and then to its present relatively more refined condition. But this refining process is never to cease.

Perhaps you will say on reading this, "What has all this to do with me? What you say may be true. But it is all too far off, too indefinite. I want something to benefit me now."

This idea of the body's regeneration is for you a benefit now, if you can accept it. It cannot be displaced from your mind. It will first, as a tiny seed, stay there. It may for months or years show no sign of life and seem to be forgotten. But it will grow and have more and more of a place in your thought. It will gradually change the quality of your thoughts. It will gradually force out an old and false interpretation of life and bring in a new one. It will impel you to look ever forward to newer joys and make you cease groping among regrets and sad remembrances of your past, when you know that such thoughts bring decay and death to the body. We are built literally of our thoughts. When we realize that our regrets, our envyings and jealousies, our borrowings of trouble, or our morbid contemplations of subjects ghastly and sickly, are literally things, and bad things, actually put in our bodies, as such thoughts, materializing themselves from invisible to visible element, turn into flesh and blood, and that as so built into ourselves they bring us pains, aches, weakness, sickness, wrinkles, bowed backs, weak knees and failing powers, we have a good and tangible reason for getting rid of them.

The body of a person given over to melancholy will be literally built of gloomy thoughts materialized into flesh and blood.

When a girl realizes more and more clearly that jealousy, peevishness, and pettish pouting moods will spoil her good looks and complexion, she will make efforts to rid herself of such thoughts. They will destroy her body. The Infinite Power for good wants all things and all people to be beautiful, healthful and symmetrical, and intends ever to increase this beauty, health, and symmetry. It works through a continual process of regeneration to keep them so. If it cannot effect such perpetual life and beauty with one physical organization, it mercifully lets it go to pieces and gives the spirit another.

When a man realizes that his angry mood, or his covetous mood, or his grumbling mood represents so much material put in his body, and that such element will give his body pain and make it sick, he has a good strong reason for having some care as to what his mind runs on, and for making the "inside of the platter clean."

Let us remember, so far as we can, that every unpleasant thought is a bad thing literally put in the body. Are some people unpleasant to us? Do their airs or affectations, or their stinginess or dishonesty, or their domineering manners, or their coarseness and vulgarity, offend us? Well, let us try and forget them. Why talk them over for an hour, holding the while all their disagreeable traits in our minds, and think of them, maybe, for hours afterwards, when we know that these unpleasant images which we carry in mind are things which are being literally put in our bodies to affect them injuriously and degenerate them? All such thoughts we must get rid of.

Such riddance is the commencement of getting a new body. It is in the way of a literal regeneration. If through long habit we find that we cannot by our own endeavor keep out of these injurious moods, if we find ourselves from time to time drawn into the current of tattle, or greed, or envy, we can cease all endeavor of our own and ask help of the Supreme Power to give us new and better thoughts. That Power, through our demand, will give us a new mind. The new mind will bring the new body